Twayne's English Authors Series

EDITOR OF THIS VOLUME

Sylvia E. Bowman

Indiana University

John Bunyan

TEAS 260

Courtesy of The British Museum, London

John Bunyan

JOHN BUNYAN

By LYNN VEACH SADLER

Bennett College

TWAYNE PUBLISHERS
A DIVISION OF G. K. HALL & CO., BOSTON

Published in 1979 by Twayne Publishers,
A Division of G. K. Hall & Co.
All Rights Reserved

Printed on permanent/durable acid-free paper and bound
in the United States of America

First Printing

Library of Congress Cataloging in Publication Data

Sadler, Lynn.
John Bunyan.

(Twayne's English authors series ; TEAS 260)
Bibliography: p. 152–59
Includes index.
1.   Bunyan, John, 1628–1688—Criticism and interpretation.
PR332.S2   1979   828'.4'07   78–26471
ISBN 0-8057-6757-6

Contents

About the Author

Mary Lynn Veach Sadler was graduated from Duke University (B.A.) *magna cum laude* and with Honors. She received the M.A. and the Ph.D. from the University of Illinois. She has held a post-doctoral research grant from the Clark Library and UCLA for work on Milton and recently earned a certificate in administration from Bryn Mawr College and Higher Education Resource Services.

She has taught at Agnes Scott College, Drake University, and North Carolina Agricultural and Technical State University. Currently, she is Chairperson of the Department of Communications and Director of the Division of Humanities at Bennett College. She received an award for "Extraordinary Undergraduate Teaching" from Drake University.

Dr. Sadler has published widely on Milton and has a forthcoming book on him. Her other publications include articles on Chaucer, Shakespeare, Greene, Lovelace, Donne, Ellison, alchemy, and the Duplin Insurrection. She has also written the Twayne volume on Thomas Carew.

She has recently turned to creative writing and has written a novella and five novels.

Preface

Anyone familiar with the outpouring of scholarship about John Bunyan will recognize that he has been claimed not only by students of literary artistry per se but by writers on allegory, emblem, sermon, fairy tale, biography, and the novel. Although he wrote some poems, Bunyan is unlikely to be sought out by critics of poetry. He has become the province of theologians and their movements, of psychologists and psychoanalysts, and of those who try to assess the combination of talent and milieu in great figures.

This diligence of Bunyan criticism can be illustrated by an allusion to an incident relating to his father. Thomas Archer, the rector of Houghton Conquest School, located several miles from Bedford and possibly the grammar school attended by John, recorded in his journal that Bunyan's father found three white rooks there. In a clever article parodying modern criticism of Kingsley Amis' *Lucky Jim,* Robert Conquest footnotes his etymology of "Bertrand" ("bright raven") in this way: "We may also be reminded of the albino rooks found by Bunyan's father in a wood near Elstow in 1634 (*Victoria History of Bedfordshire,* Vol. 3, p. 290.)."[1]

In addition to the thoroughness of Bunyan criticism, the author found herself confronting two other major problems in this study. The first, quite simply, is that most readers, having known *The Pilgrim's Progress* since childhood, tend, therefore, to dismiss Bunyan along with other "childish things." The second is more serious: the dating of events in Bunyan's life and of some of his minor works in particular is seriously snarled, and the greatest question continues to center upon Bunyan's imprisonments.[2]

The best approach to this study of Bunyan's literary contribution seemed to be to provide a brief look at Bunyan's life and times and to present summaries and assessments of the principal works, chronologically, in order to evoke closer reading of them and to develop some sense of his growth as a conscious literary artist. No attempt has been made to survey the criticism, but major critical trends and approaches are enlisted to demonstrate the variety of interpretations that Bunyan's works have prompted. Naturally, the writer is indebted to the great Bunyan critics, especially to John Brown, F. M. Harrison, Henri A. Talon, W. Y. Tindall, G. B. Harrison, and Roger Sharrock; but, wherever possible, new critical insights have been sought. This attempt is particularly true in the case of *The Holy War* and *A Book for Boys and Girls.* The former book needs, however, critical attention impossible in this kind of survey. The latter has received scant attention elsewhere, probably because it is too easily dismissed as a children's book and because it is not readily available to the reader. Hopefully, this discussion will demonstrate how valuable a work it is for its summation of so many Bunyanesque concerns.

In the analyses of *Grace Abounding,* Part I of *The Pilgrim's Progress, The Life and Death of Mr. Badman, The Holy War,* Part II of *The Pilgrim's Progress,* and *A Book for Boys and Girls,* certain recurrent interests of Bunyan and techniques of his style are pointed out. The reader should find, where they are pertinent, treatments of Bunyan's reluctance to be openly topical; the Puritan pattern of conversion he applied; his concept of self-lowliness; his emphasis on the faculties; his use of ticket-names, proverbs, and puns; his combination of everyday idiom and biblical phrase; his humor; his almost non-"Puritan" devotion to music; and his persistent criticisms of the Catholics and of other religious groups. Overall, however, the reader should find a sense of Bunyan's growth as a conscious artist and of his expanding humanity as he moved outward from himself to paint the diversity of mankind and to enjoy that diversity.

The author wishes to express her thanks to the Oxford University Press for its permission to quote from the James Blanton Wharey and Roger Sharrock edition of *The Pilgrim's Progress* and from the Sharrock edition of *Grace Abounding;* to the American Tract Society, of Oradell, New Jersey, for permission to use the E. S. Buchanan edition of *A Book for Boys and Girls;* and to the British Museum for the use of the Robert White pencil drawing of Bunyan in the Cracherode Collection.

LYNN VEACH SADLER

Bennett College

Chronology

1628 John Bunyan born in the village of Elstow, near Bedford; November 30, baptized. Later attends grammar school at Bedford or Houghton Conquest. Brought up in his father's trade of tinker.

1644 June, Mother dies; July, Margaret, his younger sister, dies; August, Bunyan's father marries his third wife. November, Bunyan pressed into service in the Parliamentary Army; garrisoned at Newport Pagnell.

1647 June, volunteers for service in Ireland; after the regiment is disbanded, Bunyan returns home without seeing active service. Marries his first wife (name unknown) sometime after his discharge.

1650 Birth of Mary, Bunyan's blind daughter. Bedford Separatist Church (later called "Bunyan Meeting") formed under the leadership of John Gifford, a major influence on Bunyan's spiritual life.

1654 Daughter Elizabeth born.

1655 Moves from Elstow to Bedford. Received into the Bedford Congregation around 1655. John Gifford dies.

1656 Begins to preach in public. Attacks the Quakers in his first work, *Some Gospel-truths Opened.*

1657 Responds to the Quaker, Edward Burrough, in *A Vindication . . . of some Gospel-truths Opened.*

1658 First wife dies; Bunyan left with four children (Mary, Elizabeth, John, Thomas). *A Few Sighs from Hell.*

1659 Marries second wife, Elizabeth. *The Doctrine of the Law and Grace Unfolded.*

1660– Imprisoned for unlicensed preaching but continues to
1672 preach, counsel, and write.

1661 August, Elizabeth pleads unsuccessfully before the judges of Bedford for release of her husband. *Profitable Meditations.*

1663 *I Will Pray with the Spirit* (second edition; first undated); *Christian Behaviour.*

166   *A Mapp shewing . . . Salvation and Damnation* (date uncertain).

1665 *One Thing Is Needful* (date uncertain); *The Holy City; Prison Meditations; The Resurrection of the Dead.*

1666 *Grace Abounding,* a spiritual autobiography; *A Christian Dialogue* (between 1666 and 1672).

1672 January 21, ratified as pastor of the Bedford Separatist Church. May 9, licensed as a Congregational preacher. *A Confession of My Faith; A New and Useful Concordance to the Holy Bible* (perhaps earlier); *A Defence of the Doctrine of Justification, By Faith in Jesus Christ.* Released from prison.

1673 *Differences in Judgment About Water Baptism, No Bar to Communion; The Barren Fig-tree* (date uncertain).

1674 Accused of helping Agnes Beaumont murder her father. *Peaceable Principles and True; Reprobation Asserted* (date and work uncertain).

1675 *Light for Them That Sit in Darkness; Instruction for the Ignorant.*

1676 *Saved by Grace; The Strait Gate.*

1677 Second imprisonment for about six months, probably during the first half of 1677, for not attending the parish church.

1678 *The Pilgrim's Progress* (Part I); *Come and Welcome, to Jesus Christ.*

1679 *A Treatise of the Fear of God.*

1680 *The Life and Death of Mr. Badman.*

1682 *The Holy War.*

1683 *The Greatness of the Soul; A Case of Conscience Resolved.*

1684 *A Holy Life the Beauty of Christianity; Seasonable Counsel...; The Pilgrim's Progress* (Part II); *A Caution to Stir Up to Watch against Sin* (date uncertain).

1685 *A Discourse Upon the Pharisee and the Publicane; Questions About ... the Seventh-Day Sabbath.*

1686 *A Book for Boys and Girls.*

1688 *The Jerusalem Sinner Saved; The Advocateship of Jesus Christ; A Discourse of the ... House of God; The Water of Life; Solomon's Temple Spiritualiz'd.* August 19, last sermon. August 31, dies and is buried at Bunhill Fields, London.

1689 *The Acceptable Sacrifice; Mr. John Bunyan's Last Sermon.*

1692 Death of Elizabeth Bunyan. Published for the first time: *An Exposition of the First Ten Chapters of Genesis; Of Jus-*

tification By An Imputed Righteousness; Paul's Departure and Crown; Of the Trinity, and a Christian; Of the Law, and a Christian; Israel's Hope Encouraged; The Desires of the Righteous Granted; The Saint's Priviledge and Profit; Christ A Compleat Saviour; The Saint's Knowledge of Christ's Love; A Discourse Of the House of the Forest of Lebanon; Of Antichrist, and His Ruine.

CHAPTER 1

Bunyan's Life, Milieu, and Works

I *Early Life and First Marriage*

THE facts of John Bunyan's life remain obscure. He was born in the village of Elstow, near Bedford, in the Midlands of England, in 1628. His birth date is unknown, but he was baptized on November 30. He is thought to have attended grammar school at Bedford or at Houghton Conquest, near Bedford. Though his family had once been landed yeomen, Bunyan and his father were braziers, whitesmiths, or, according to the term later used by John's second wife, "tinkers." His deriders therefore listed him among the "mechanicks"; that is, he was one of the self-made, often illiterate Puritan preachers who followed manual trades. This label, however, was to produce from Bunyan not only pride, but a pun:

> For I'm no poet, nor a poet's son,
> But a mechanic, guided by no rule
> But what I gained in a grammar school
> In my minority. . . .[1]

The next concrete information known about Bunyan belongs to the year 1644, when a series of crises rapidly befell him: his mother died in June; his younger sister, Margaret, died in July; and his father married for the third time in August. In November of the same year, Bunyan was pressed into service in the Parliamentary Army that was opposing his father's own Royalist side. Garrisoned at Newport Pagnell, which was very close to his home, Bunyan was under the governorship of Sir Samuel Luke. Luke was destined to be satirized in *Hudibras,* the work of his secretary, Samuel Butler, and a work which reveals how adversely Puritans and mechanics could be viewed. While at Newport Pagnell, Bunyan could have

heard the preaching of the General Baptist, Henry Denne; and his
future conversion to the faith of the Baptists may, unconsciously,
have begun this early. In June, 1647, Bunyan volunteered for service in Ireland and was about to embark when his regiment was disbanded. He returned home without seeing active service.

After his discharge, Bunyan married his first wife, whose name is
not known. Some critics conjecture that she was "Mary," the name
of the Bunyans' blind daughter, who was born in 1650. In *Grace
Abounding,* written years later during his first imprisonment,
Bunyan revealed that, although his wife was poor, her "dowry"
came to be worth more to him than money and goods. She told him
stories about her godly father and shared with him two books that
were to exert a great influence on his spiritual and literary life:
Arthur Dent's *The Plaine Mans Pathway to Heaven* (1601) and
Bishop Lewis Bayley's *The Practice of Piety* (1612). When Mrs.
Bunyan died in 1658, she left her husband with four children
(Mary, Elizabeth, John, and Thomas).

II   *John Gifford and the Bedford Congregation*

Another major influence on Bunyan's life came in 1651–1653
when he made his first contact with John Gifford and the Separatist Church of Bedford. Gifford, who had been a Royalist major,
was sentenced to death for his participation in an uprising in Kent
in 1648. With the help of his sister, he escaped from prison and hid
overnight in a ditch. He then established himself as a physician in
Bedford, led the life of a profligate, and was at last converted to
Puritanism. He founded the Bedford Church in 1650; and he and
his successor as its pastor, John Burton, were moderate Baptists
who did not demand baptism as a condition for joining the congregation. Gifford's church was later called "Bunyan meeting" in
testimony to Bunyan's close association with it.

Among the Puritan sectarians, the fear of reprobation and hell
that was aroused by zealous preachers could cause not only trauma
but the religious melancholy described in Robert Burton's *Anatomy of Melancholy.* Those who had experienced conversion were
expected to detail for others their frequent lapses into despair and
their ultimate success. No doubt John Gifford, from his pulpit,
told all who would listen about his own "case of conscience," as
such experiences of conversion from reprobation were called. Bunyan followed this established practice in a personal way in *Grace*

Abounding and in a much more formal way in *The Pilgrim's Progress* and other works. The genesis of his literary works is thus to be found in his Puritan religious experience. When he joined the Bedford Congregation sometime around 1655, his most intense temptations to despair of salvation were in the offing. Like other Puritans in the throes of conversion, he searched the Bible for messages sent to him alone; only later was he able to adapt his situation to the needs of all "pilgrims."

When Gifford died in 1655, Bunyan had already spoken before the Bedford brethren; in 1656, he began to preach publicly. Much of his time was also given to visiting church members and potential converts in the villages around Bedford. Proof of his growing importance in Gifford's church is provided by the family move from Elstow to Bedford in 1655 after his blind daughter Mary and his daughter Elizabeth, who was born in 1654, had been baptized in Elstow.

III *Bunyan and Puritanism*

Bunyan was already undergoing a spiritual crisis when he encountered John Gifford. His parents had not been Dissenters but regular members of the Church of England; and the satisfaction he derived from such sports as "tip-cat" and bell ringing, as described in *Grace Abounding,* pictures an England that could still be merry and nonpuritanical. The Anglicans tended to stress reasonableness in their religious commitments, as indeed their church of the Middle Way (the *via media*) proclaimed. Accordingly, they could accept as religious authority sources other than the Bible itself. One of Bunyan's early spiritual tasks was weaning himself from the rather liberal ways of his father's Anglican household to the harsher and more conservative atmosphere of Puritanism.

The Puritans relied on the Bible alone, found all men sinners, and knew that salvation was earned by no man — no matter how godly he might be — but was achieved only through Jesus' grace. The route to salvation through grace came to be carefully prescribed in a classic Puritan pattern that is essentially the path charted for Bunyan's own experience in *Grace Abounding:* conviction of sin; vocation or calling, during which the candidate received some assurance that he was among the elect; justification through a "saving faith"; sanctification in the godly life; and glorification, the consummation of the process when the Christian soldier and wayfarer found God. Like the rhythm of Scripture, where the children of God fall away from and are recalled to Him, this conversion process alternated despair and hope.

In the general sense of the Puritanism outlined above, Bunyan is a "Puritan"; yet he himself disliked labels and displayed both similarities to and differences from the historical English Puritans. In fact, Bunyan's own Puritanism shares the medieval zeal for reformation and simplicity of the Wycliffites, of Chaucer's parson and plowman, and of William Langland's *Piers Plowman*. Indeed, Bunyan's independence in religious views is characteristic of the sometimes querulous and always energetic history of the Puritan movement.

Not until the late sixteenth century did Puritanism assume a formal structure. At first applied contemptuously to those who felt that the Elizabethan Compromise, Anglicanism, was still too much like Roman Catholicism, the term "Puritan" came to be used for the followers of John Calvin, who preached predestination and who emphasized, just as Bunyan later did, grace as the only means of salvation. The Calvinists believed that they could work through the state to establish God's community on earth; and their Presbyterian offshoot founded its government on a political model: the ministers were chosen by the people and in turn selected an assembly of "presbyters." The splinter groups or sects who broke away from the Calvinists — and to whom Bunyan was to belong — believed that their destiny lay outside of the state in small communities of the holy.

During the reign of Queen Elizabeth, the Puritan movement had been largely intellectual. Centered at the University of Cambridge, it could claim to have influenced such poet-scholars as Edmund Spenser. Elizabeth's administration had perhaps spent too much energy on the Catholics to mount great opposition against any Puritan voices except vociferous extremists like Stephen Gosson, who wrote against the corruption of poets and players, or like Martin Marprelate, the pseudonym of the pamphleteer who condemned the government for restraining the press. James I, on the other hand, felt that kingship itself was threatened by the Puritan opposition to the office of bishops. The extravagance of the court of Charles I and his Catholic queen, Henrietta Maria, and the increasingly "high-church" Anglicanism of Archbishop William Laud, seen by the Puritans as a return to the trappings of Catholicism, exacerbated the conflict that was to come to a head with the outbreak of civil war in 1642, the war of which Bunyan became a part.

That war divided not only the country against itself, Royalist (Bunyan's father, for one) against Puritan (the side Bunyan was drafted to serve), but Puritan against Puritan. Long before the actual hostilities, the demand for preachers and pastors to help individuals who were seeking assurance of election to salvation had made Puritanism less an intellectual and more a popular movement. The way was opened for the rise of additional sectarians and separatists, who would divide over the way to salvation.

Around 1580–1581, Robert Browne founded the sect known as Independents, Congregationalists, or "Brownists," some of whom went to Holland. Refinements were made; and one result was the establishment of the Anabaptists or, later, "Baptists," who fostered baptism for adult believers. In 1609, John Smith "separated" from the Amsterdam congregation by baptizing himself. A Baptist church was established at Leyden, and Thomas Helwys returned to England to found a Baptist community whose members became known as General Baptists from their rejection of Calvinistic election and from their belief in "general" salvation. The Particular or Calvinist Baptists, who soon outnumbered the General Baptists, came into existence in 1616. Both groups were in agreement about such ordinary Puritan concerns as opposition to the "Popish" trappings and ceremonies of the Anglican Church and to the Book of Common Prayer (the latter an especial concern of John Bunyan). Unlike mainline Puritans, however, they demanded separation of church and state. They also opposed tithes, stood for total liberty of conscience, and denounced a clergy trained by the universities. In their pulpits were mostly tinkers (like Bunyan), cobblers, and other "mechanicks"; for the preachers, as well as the congregations, were from the lower classes. On the extreme left beyond these Baptists were such fanatics as Fifth Monarchists, Muggletonians, and Ranters. The Civil War brought differences of opinion among all types of Puritans, for example, Presbyterians versus Independents; but most were united against this extreme left wing, especially against the Fifth Monarchists.

By 1653, England was a commonwealth under the Puritan rule of Oliver Cromwell; and the Bedford sectarians were a part of the state church. Under the Protectorate, except for the Quakers and the Fifth Monarchists, there was little strictly religious persecution of those who were "Puritans." Still, in 1657, in response to a rumor that Cromwell would become king, the Bedford Congregation sent a petition to Whitehall Palace voicing its opposition.

In the welter of Puritan sects, Bunyan cannot be simply categorized relative to his own "opinion." Though he is generally called a "Puritan," he was not content, as were mainline Puritans, to seek reform of the Established (Anglican) Church. He at one point proclaimed himself an "Anabaptist," but he is widely referred to now as a "Particular Open Communion Baptist," one who was liberal about the methods of baptism and about church membership.[2] He continued to display his reluctance to be confined within a group by renewing in Part II of *The Pilgrim's Progress* his disagreements with more exacting Baptists over "special" and "general" calls to salvation. Even Bunyan's mainly *literary* works call attention to the fatuousness of those who worry more about labels and doctrinal minutia than about the grace that can lead *Man* to God. For example, in *The Pilgrim's Progress,* Bunyan uses characters to satirize different groups: the Anglicans in Worldly Wise-man, Formalist, and Hypocrisy; the Latitudinarians in By-ends; the Deists and the Quakers in Ignorance; and the Quakers in Error.

Bunyan persistently viewed himself as avoiding petty arguments: "I never cared to meddle with things that were controverted, and in dispute amongst the Saints, especially things of the lowest nature; yet it pleased me much to contend with great earnestness for the Word of Faith, and the remission of sins by the Death and Sufferings of Jesus: but I say, as to other things, I should let them alone, because I saw they engendered strife...."[3] In fact, he scoffed at all carping sects and preferred to be inscribed simply as a "Christian." In *The Holy City,* Bunyan is looking forward to the establishment of the New Jerusalem when there will be no doctrine or preachers but the "doctrine of the twelve": "It shall not be then as now, a Popish doctrine, a Quaker's doctrine, a prelatical doctrine, and the Presbyter, Independent, and Anabaptist, thus distinguished, and thus confounding and destroying."[4] A similar disparagement appears in Bunyan's *A Holy Life:* "It is strange to see at this day how, notwithstanding all the threatenings of God, men are wedded to their own opinions, beyond what the law of grace and love will admit. Here is a Presbyter, here is an Independent, and a Baptist, so joined each man to his own opinion, that they cannot have that communion one with another, as by the testimony of the Lord Jesus they are commanded and enjoined."[5] Bunyan seems always to have felt that all ways can be God's and that many roads can lead to Him — so long as one does not omit the central fact of the indispensability of grace, the only tenet that must be maintained at all costs.

The strange combination of independence and of a dislike of disputes resulted in a dearth of topical references in Bunyan's works, though many argue that he simply masked his thrusts in allegory. The directly controversial tracts, however, are a poor match for John Milton's vituperation. Bunyan's castigation of the follies of his period is, for example, kept very general throughout *A Holy Life* and in the preface to *The Jerusalem Sinner Saved:* "The nation doth swarm with vile ones *now,* as ever it did since it was a nation."[6] Like many of the sectarians of his period, he was a millenarian, one who awaited the establishment of Christ's kingdom on earth; but Bunyan was always careful to affirm his allegiance to the temporal power, notably in *A Discourse Of The House of the Forest of Lebanon* and in *Of Antichrist.* He seemed to feel that the government would be able to work with the kingdom of Christ.

IV *Writer, Preacher, and Controversialist*

Conventicles, the sectarian religious assemblies, regularly appointed controversialists to represent them in doctrinal disputes. Bunyan, despite his aversion to the fine art of bickering, was now of such stature that he undertook this task for the Bedford Congregation. The outpouring of his approximately sixty works[7] began with *Some Gospel-truths Opened* (1656) and *A Vindication of Some Gospel-truths Opened* (1657); both of these works are directed against the Quakers, who, though they shared many views with the Baptists, were seen as a major rival and were often accused of appropriating Baptist doctrines. In 1658, Bunyan produced *A Few Sighs from Hell,* a hellfire-and-brimstone piece that used the biblical parable of Lazarus and the rich man as an object lesson for sinners.

Bunyan rapidly gained fame as a preacher and was occasionally invited to address the congregations of Pinner's Hall, the London gathering place for Dissenters. Like other unordained "mechanic" preachers, he was frequently attacked as "unlicensed" and "unlearned" by clergymen trained at the university. These attacks were as likely to come from fellow Puritans as from Anglicans. In May, 1659, for example, when he was preaching in a barn in Toft, Cambridgeshire, his right to preach at all was questioned by the Reverend Thomas Smith, a Puritan who was professor of Arabic at Cambridge and librarian of the university. Another learned Puritan, William Dell, master of Caius College, Cambridge, and rector of Yelden, however, with much personal risk, invited Bunyan to preach on Christmas, 1659. Dell's parishioners were so angered that they petitioned the House of Lords against their pastor.

Many apparently shared Dell's admiration for Bunyan. When Charles II asked Doctor John Owen how a learned man could listen to such an illiterate preacher, Owen's answer was that he would surrender all his learning for Bunyan's power of preaching. There is another report of a Cambridge student who came to jeer a Bunyan sermon and left a convert. Similarly, the epithet, "Bishop Bunyan," which had been a taunt, eventually turned into praise. Bunyan's fame is also demonstrated by this anonymous ballad verse:

> There's a moderate Doctour at Cripplegate dwells,
> Whom Smythes, his curate, at trimming excells;
> But Bunyan, a tinker, hath tickled his gills.

Bunyan's next work, *The Doctrine of the Law and Grace Unfolded,* on the covenant between God and man, and the last one before his imprisonment, was published in 1659. It is particularly important for the brief sketch it contains of his own experience as a sinner. He had been preaching for some two years by this time and had focused in his sermons principally on the sins of man. Now feeling some spiritual comfort, he began to preach of deliverance through Christ's blood and to call on his audiences to pray for him.

In the same year, 1659, that he was engaged with his fellow Puritans, the Reverends Smith and Dell, Bunyan married his second wife, Elizabeth, who was to survive him by a year and a half and who presented him with two more children, Sarah and Joseph. All of Bunyan's children, except blind Mary, outlived him.

V *Bunyan During the First Imprisonment*

Despite Bunyan's disinclination to be disputatious and anarchical, his life seemed to advance inexorably toward conflict with the civil authorities. Bunyan generally approved of the Puritan Cromwell; and, with Gifford, he signed a Bedfordshire document sent to the Lord Protector applauding his actions and recommending two county magistrates to the Assembly. But, although Cromwell favored full religious toleration, he had been forced to declare for Presbyterianism to placate the Scots. Ironically, it was the exiled Charles who promised full liberty of conscience in the Declaration of Breda (1660). With the restoration of the kingship in that same year, however, fear of treason and rumors of the Anabaptist riots in Münster brought repression to Dissenters. Marvelous tales of their midnight baptisms and secret conventicles and conclaves in abandoned barns began to arouse government spies. The authorities are hardly to be blamed for fearing all sects with the horror that belonged to only one of the smallest groups, the Fifth Monarchists, who had, under the leadership of Thomas Venner, produced a riot in London in 1661. The stage was set for Bunyan's persecution. The Bedford Congregation seemed to anticipate the coming troubles; for, just prior to the Restoration, it designated a day of prayer for the nation.

Although Bunyan talks of his imprisonment in *Grace Abounding,* in keeping with the general spirit of that work, he provides few details. Not until the publication in 1765 of *A Relation of the Imprisonment of Mr. John Bunyan,* a manuscript passed down in the Bunyan family, did his full account of the story become known.[8]

This work relates how, on November 12, 1660, after Bunyan had been preaching for about five years, he was warned that Justice Francis Wingate, the magistrate of the village of Samsell in Bedfordshire, who was seeking his first case, had heard of Bunyan's intention to preach there. Against the advice of his friends and after much debate with himself, Bunyan carried through his intention, reasoning that he must set an example of strength for his parishioners. When he was arrested, the justice was not at home, and a friend pledged his security. On the following morning, Bunyan appeared before the constable and Justice Wingate; and the presiding officer was surprised to hear that no weapons had been confiscated. After Bunyan had admitted that he would break bond to preach again, he was sentenced to the county jail in Bedford until quarter-sessions (court held quarterly by the county justice of the peace). While he awaited the completion of his "mittimus" or warrant, Doctor William Lindall parried words with him.

As Bunyan was on his way to jail, two friends secured a promise from the magistracy that he would be released if he would but "say

some certain words" (that he would not preach any more). Waiting
again for the justice, Bunyan encountered Wingate's brother-in-
law, Lawyer William Foster, who also suggested that Bunyan had
only to promise to preach no more in order to be set free. Foster
insisted, moreover, that Bunyan could not understand Scripture
because he did not know Greek. Still, Bunyan remained adamant
before Wingate and Foster; and he was kept in jail some days while
his friends applied, unsuccessfully, to get Justice Crompton of
Elstow to take bond for him.

After seven weeks of incarceration, Bunyan was tried in January,
1661, at the quarter-sessions in Bedford. He disputed with a party
of justices about the recently reinstated Anglican Book of Common
Prayer, and he heard Justice John Keeling's great inaccuracy —
that this document had been in use since the time of the Apostles!
Ignorant of the law, if not ignorant of the Bible, Bunyan did not
understand that explanations in lieu of a plea constituted a pronouncement of guilt — or so Justice Wingate afterward presented
the case. Bunyan again refused to conform to the Anglican Church
and admitted that he would preach if he were freed, and he was
again remanded to jail.

So quickly had the Royalists rallied after the Restoration that
there had been no time to complete the Act of Uniformity according to which Bunyan should have been brought to trial. Instead he
was accused under a revived statute, the "35th of Elizabeth,"
which was originally used against the Nonconformists who chose to
attend conventicles rather than their parish churches. The first
offense against this law carried a penalty of three months'
imprisonment. At the end of three months, Paul Cobb, the clerk of
the peace, visited Bunyan for the justices to admonish him to submit to the Established Church. Bunyan could not be prevailed upon
to conform or to abandon the pulpit, but he vowed his loyalty to
his prince and offered to submit the notes of his sermons as proof
that he preached no heresy: "...For I do sincerly desire to live
quietly in my country, and submit to the present authority."⁹ Because of his refusal to agree to Cobb's proposals, however, Bunyan
remained in jail.

In accordance with custom, many prisoners received their freedom at the coronation of Charles II on April 23, 1661. Again, John
Bunyan seemed fated: the technicality that he had not *sued for* pardon prevented his release. Then, not being allowed to appear himself at the assizes or court session of August, 1661, Bunyan sent his

wife Elizabeth with a petition for the judges. She had tried unsuccessfully at the House of Lords in London to get him released; and, on the advice of one "Lord Barkwood," she had returned to petition the local officials. After many failures to gain access, she appeared before them in the Swan Chamber of a Bedford inn. Elizabeth, who had been married to Bunyan not fully two years, who was stepmother to his four children, and who had lost the child she had been carrying when she heard of his arrest, defended her husband eloquently: "...because he is a Tinker, and a poor man; therefore he is despised, and cannot have justice."[10] Although she was unsuccessful in obtaining John's release, her defense won the pity and friendship of Sir Matthew Hale, who supplied legal advice and suggestions as to where she might next ply her case.

Another attempt to win freedom during the spring assizes of 1662 was equally unsuccessful. When Bunyan tried to get himself included among a group who had completed their sentences and were to be released, Clerk Cobb saw that his name was removed from consideration. Although Bunyan continued in jail, he was apparently provided relaxed conditions until higher authorities discovered that he had actually been permitted to go to London, where he had helped some Baptists. At this point, Bunyan's jailer was reprimanded; and Bunyan became a close prisoner.

Though he continued to hope in vain for trial and release, Bunyan appears in his *Prison Meditations* to have had at least as much stamina and fortitude as the Cavalier poet, Richard Lovelace, in "To Althea from Prison." Bunyan's mind is attuned to Christ:

> I am, indeed, in prison now
> In body, but my mind
> Is free to study Christ, and how
> Unto me he is kind.
>
> For though men keep my outward man
> Within their locks and bars,
> Yet by the faith of Christ I can
> Mount higher than the stars.
>
> Their *fetters* cannot *spirits* tame,
> Nor tie up God from me;
> My faith and hope they cannot lame,
> Above them I shall be.[11]

Bunyan's first imprisonment lasted twelve years, although an earlier (unsubstantiated) theory claims that he was released for a short
while in 1666. His activities during this period included preaching,
counseling, publishing, and making "tagg'd laces" to sell. He may
also have written most of Part I of *The Pilgrim's Progress* at this
time.

In 1661, Bunyan published *Profitable Meditations,* a poetic
"conference between Christ and a sinner." The major literary value
of this first prison production is that it provides a hint for the figure
of Apollyon in *The Pilgrim's Progress.* In 1663,[12] Bunyan brought
out the second edition of *I Will Pray with the Spirit,* which was
about the spontaneity of prayer, whose *living* qualities Bunyan
stresses, and which was in opposition to the set patterns of the
Anglican Book of Common Prayer. It was probably composed during the six months of relative freedom between the autumn and
spring assizes of 1661–1662. In 1663 also appeared *Christian
Behaviour,* Bunyan's typical Puritan guide to God-pleasing conduct for husbands, wives, parents, children, masters, servants, and
others.

The broadside, *A Mapp shewing . . . Salvation and Damnation,*
is now generally dated 1664. *One Thing Is Needful,* on death, judgment, heaven, and hell, is thought to have appeared first in 1665.[13]
In that year *did* appear *The Holy City,* a vision of the New Jerusalem characteristic of Puritan literature; *Prison Meditations,* in
verse; and *The Resurrection of the Dead.* In 1666 came Bunyan's
great spiritual autobiography, *Grace Abounding.* Introspective in
the extreme, it yet fulfills the Puritan injunctions first to put one-
self right with God and then to help one's brethren. No copy of *A
Christian Dialogue* is extant, but it was probably published between
1666 and 1672.[14] Likewise, no copy of *A New and Useful Concordance to the Holy Bible* is known; but this work is generally believed to have been published by 1672 and perhaps a little earlier.[15]

The year 1672 also brought renewed doctrinal disputes. Bunyan's
A Confession of My Faith opposed stricter London Baptists who
demanded baptism by dipping as a condition of communion. The
Anglican Church, under the spokesmanship of Edward Fowler,
who believed that man could reachieve his prelapsarian perfection,
came under attack in Bunyan's *A Defence of the Doctrine of Justification, By Faith in Jesus Christ.*

As his output of works in prison indicates, Bunyan was not un-
duly restrained during these twelve years. Nor was he particularly

singled out for repression. The 1660s allowed little respite for any Dissenters, hounded as they were by the legislation of Edward Hyde, the Earl of Clarendon and Charles II's Chancellor of the Exchequer. The Act of Uniformity of 1662 crushed those who would accept neither the Book of Common Prayer nor the ordination of bishops of the Established Church. The Conventicle Act of 1664 levied fines against or imprisoned those found guilty of illegal assembly. But, by the expiration of this act in 1668, Clarendon himself, threatened with impeachment for treason, had fallen upon evil days and had fled to France in 1667. Bunyan probably again enjoyed something like a parole.

The Bedford Church Book contains no entries for approximately five and one-half years during the heaviest of the persecution of the 1660s; but the fact that it records Bunyan's ratification as pastor on January 21, 1672, a date before his release from prison, illustrates the decline of *civil* restrictions. Taking advantage of the moment, he secured a license to preach, under the heading *Congregational,* on May 9, 1672; and he urged his brethren to purchase the barn of Josias Ruffhead for a church. Ironically, however, *ecclesiastical* controls became more active and were to affect Bunyan's future.

With the Declaration of Indulgence in 1672, many of those imprisoned for their faith began to sue for release. Another of the oddities of Bunyan's life is that his was one of the few non-Quaker names in the application that brought his freedom in September, 1672. His return to freedom and to the pastoral demands on his time did not slow the surge of doctrinal works from his hand. Another expression of his liberal attitude toward baptism appeared in 1673 in *Differences in Judgment About Water Baptism, No Bar to Communion.* That same year[16] may also have produced *The Barren Fig-tree,* which employs a constant Bunyan theme, the fruitless "professor" of religion (one who professes to be religious).

VI *Bunyan and Agnes Beaumont*

One of the most amazing episodes of Bunyan's career is his entanglement in the life of a parishioner, Agnes Beaumont, in 1674. This twenty-one-year-old daughter of John Beaumont of Edworth had joined the Baptist congregation of Gamlingay, a village near Bedford, against her father's wishes. In February, she had planned to attend the Gamlingay meeting, but the horseman engaged by her brother to take her there failed to appear. After much altercation, the brother managed to persuade Bunyan to allow Agnes to ride behind him to the assembly. Gossipers carried the news to the father; and the pair was also so unfortunate as to be seen by a Bedford clergyman, the Reverend Lane, who later slandered them. They arrived at the meeting without incident; and Agnes found it, as anticipated, a "feast of ffatt things."

Bunyan was not returning in the direction of her home, but Agnes at length found another ride. When she arrived again in Edworth, her father refused to let her in and expelled her from the house until she promised to stop following the preaching of Bunyan. After she had spent the night in the barn, Agnes went to her brother's until a reconciliation was effected. But, soon after her return home, her father mysteriously died. Her rejected suitor, Lawyer Farrow, accused Agnes of murdering Mr. Beaumont with poison provided by Bunyan. She was brought to trial but was found innocent and later wrote her story in her own words.[17] In light of this incident, the additions to *Grace Abounding* of Bunyan's protests that he is innocent of trafficking with women are certainly comprehensible.

VII *Works, 1674–1676*

Despite the frustrations of these times, Bunyan published, probably in 1674, *Peaceable Principles and True* and, according to Charles Doe, the editor of the folio edition of the *Works, Reprobation Asserted.* The former again dealt with the problem of baptism, and the latter remains a repudiable work.[18] Against the Quakers, Bunyan brought forth, in 1675, *Light for Them that Sit in Darkness.* The same year produced *Instruction for the Ignorant,* which is in the form of a catechism and is related to the argument over communion. *Saved by Grace* was published in 1676.[19] *The Strait Gate,* also appearing in 1676, is an important work, particularly from a literary point of view, for its "talkatives" and "formalists" in religion offer comparison with characters in *The Pilgrim's Progress.*

VIII *The Second Imprisonment*

The repeal of the Declaration of Indulgence in 1675 brought repression of conventicles and the renewal of persecution. By March, 1675, a *civil* warrant had been issued by the county magistrates for Bunyan's arrest; but somehow no arrest was made. He was again imprisoned, however, for about six months, probably during the first half of 1677. The reasons given are at variance: for unlicensed preaching; on the ecclesiastical charge that he had failed to attend communion at St. Cuthbert's Church in Bedford; and upon his neglect of a summons to appear before the archdeacon's court as a Nonconformist. Apparently, after he failed to answer the *ecclesiastical* court summons for not attending his parish church, he was finally arrested and imprisoned, again in the county jail[20] in Bedford. The bond for his release is dated June 21, 1677.

His old enemy, William Foster, of Bedford, had secured the writ for his arrest; but his friend, John Owen, the leader of the Independents, effected his release. Two members of the congregation of George Cokayne bonded themselves for his good behavior. Cokayne was pastor of an Open Communion Baptist church in London and had become Bunyan's friend when the "tinker," although still maintaining his ties with Bedford, began to preach more and more in Baptist pulpits of the capital city after 1672.

Short though it was, this imprisonment was monumental in Bunyan's literary life. Critics now generally believe that he completed Part I of *The Pilgrim's Progress* during this period. It was published in 1678, as was *Come and Welcome, to Jesus Christ* (on John 6:37), and shows how far Bunyan had been weaned from the self-preoccupation of *Grace Abounding*.

IX   *The Postimprisonment Days*

Bunyan published in 1679 *A Treatise of the Fear of God,* a work that presents, incidentally, his liberal attitudes toward church singing. Two of Bunyan's major literary works, *The Life and Death of Mr. Badman* and *The Holy War,* appeared in 1680 and 1682, respectively. *Badman,* in dialogue form, is a social commentary. *The Holy War,* an allegory of the struggle of the forces of Good and Evil for man's soul, reveals another approach to the human pilgrimage toward God. In content and form, it challenges comparison with *The Pilgrim's Progress.*

The Greatness of the Soul, an enlargement of a sermon preached at Pinner's Hall in London, was published in 1683. The same year forced Bunyan to deny the request of the Bedford women that they be allowed to hold separate meetings. In view of Bunyan's liberal attitude toward so many church matters, such as communion and baptism, this stance is surprising; and the work, *A Case of Conscience Resolved,* is an intriguing one.

The year 1684 produced *A Holy Life the Beauty of Christianity; Seasonable Counsel: Or, Advice to Sufferers;* and, perhaps, another broadside, *A Caution to Stir Up to Watch against Sin.*[21] The chief work of this year, however, is the continuation (Part II) of *The Pilgrim's Progress;* but this time the allegory centers on the pilgrimage of Christiana, Christian's wife, and illustrates a constant Bunyanesque theme: that the ways to God are many and His pilgrims varied. Another constant theme of Bunyan, obedience to the Law in the "carnal" stage of the Puritan conversion, is put forth in *A Discourse Upon the Pharisee and the Publicane* (1685). In the same year, Bunyan opposed keeping the Jewish Sabbath, Saturday, in *Questions About . . . the Seventh-Day Sabbath.*

Two imprisonments made Bunyan wary. The reign of James II, a Catholic, brought more difficulties for Dissenters and anticipating the worst, Bunyan, in December, 1685, drew up a deed of gift so that his wife would have his property in the event of his third imprisonment. This document lay undiscovered until Bunyan's St. Cuthbert's Street cottage in Bedford was torn down in 1838. The worst did not occur; Bunyan, with other Dissenters, found himself being cultivated by James II, who tried to help his fellow Catholics by expanding toleration. Though Bunyan refused patronage for himself, he did secure political preferment for some members of his church.

Such worries about his continued freedom are almost belied by the publication of one of the most unusual of Bunyan's "literary" works, *A Book for Boys and Girls* (1686). The overall playfulness of this collection of emblem poems seems to suggest that the author's mind was at peace. In it, Bunyan again illustrates that the ways to God are many and that His pilgrims are as varied as the creatures featured in the poems.

In the year of his death, 1688, Bunyan published *The Jerusalem Sinner Saved* (also referred to as *Good News for the Vilest of Men*); *The Advocateship of Jesus Christ* (also referred to as *The Work of Jesus Christ as an Advocate*); *A Discourse of the . . . House of God,* on fruitful "professors" of religion; *The Water of Life,* another work on the dominant Bunyan theme of Christ's grace; and *Solomon's Temple Spiritualiz'd.* The last is Bunyan's most consistently typological work and one that deserves more attention from critics interested in seventeenth-century typology.

Bunyan delivered his final sermon on August 19, 1688. He had already committed himself to preach it when a young neighbor sought his aid in bringing reconciliation with the boy's father, who had threatened disinheritance. Journeying to London to give the sermon, Bunyan rode out of his way to Reading to see this man; and he managed to persuade the father to receive his son once again. Bunyan then left to ride the forty miles to London. The rainstorms he encountered induced a fever; and Bunyan fell sick, though he preached as promised. Twelve days later, on August 31, 1688, he died at the home of John Strudwick and was buried in the London Nonconformist cemetery of Bunhill Fields.

X   The Remaining Works

Mr. John Bunyan's Last Sermon, on John 1:13, was published in 1689, as was *The Acceptable Sacrifice,* on the "contrite heart." Charles Doe, Bunyan's first editor and his biographer, brought out a folio edition of his works in 1692 and printed the following ones for the first time: *An Exposition of the First Ten Chapters of Genesis; Of Justification By An Imputed Righteousness; Paul's Departure and Crown,* on 2 Timothy 4:6–8; *Of the Trinity, and a Christian; Of the Law, and a Christian; Israel's Hope Encouraged,* on the difference between hope and faith; *The Desires of the Righteous Granted; The Saint's Priviledge and Profit; Christ A Compleat Saviour; The Saint's Knowledge of Christ's Love; A Discourse Of the House of the Forest of Lebanon* (typological); and *Of Antichrist, and His Ruine.* Doe also published Bunyan's *The Heavenly Foot-man* in 1698. This work is particularly important, for its presentation of the "ways" to be run and of the "marks" to be followed by those who journey toward heaven offers comparison once again with *The Pilgrim's Progress.*

XI   The Dearth of Early Editions of Bunyan's Works

The rarity of early editions of Bunyan's works is the result of two strangely similar events. Many of his earlier pieces were published by Francis "Elephant" Smith, who was often at odds with the government for dealing with Nonconformist authors. Smith's warehouse near Temple Bar was searched; and many books were seized by Roger L'Estrange, Charles II's censor. The Great Fire of London, in 1666, destroyed most of the confiscated books, including those of Bunyan. In 1865, fire also destroyed many of Bunyan's works that had been collected by his early editor, George Offor, and arranged for auction in London. The sale was to last eleven days, beginning Tuesday, June 27; but, by Thursday, the fire had broken out. What was left of the some four thousand items was purchased by an American agent for three hundred pounds.

XII   *The Popular Figure*

As Bunyan's reputation grew, legends about him spread apace. Probably because he was an itinerant tinker and because of his travels to remote counties, he was endowed with Gypsy origins by some of his earliest critics. The anonymous *An Account of the Life and Actions of John Bunyan* identified him as a Royalist present at the siege of Leicester led by Prince Rupert. A newssheet brought off a great piece of wit by advertising Bunyan's *A Few Sighs From Hell; Or, The Groans of a Damned Soul* beneath the announcement of Cromwell's death. Charles II also displayed a facetious bent by having this same work bound with a salacious French romance and put in his library. And the humor that is so much a part of Bunyan's personality spurts forth in the famous answer to the constable who overtook him with a warrant as Bunyan was traveling disguised as a waggoner. The response to the query of whether he knew that "devil of a fellow Bunyan" was this: "Know him. You might well call him a devil if you knew him as well as I once did."

Even images of Bunyan's life in prison produced an exceedingly romantic and popular effect: he supported his family by making "tagg'd laces"; his blind daughter carried him a jug of soup daily; he fashioned a flute from the rail of a prison stool and burned its holes with a candle. Artifacts in the Bunyan Museum in Bedford exude a strange compound of truth and legend; for example, the tinker's homemade anvil and his "iron fiddle" — made of thin iron plates and as large as a full-sized Italian violin.[22] A popular anecdote relates that Bunyan was forced to turn over his tools, including the anvil, to cover his debts to an Elstow innkeeper.

The great legend about Bunyan, however, has been that he was an unnurtured genius, a view that he helped to foster. Like other members of the religious sects of his era, he seems to have held his lack of more than a grammar-school education — in itself rather unusual for a family of the Bunyan rank — as a distinction; for he probably shared the view that "school" knowledge could deaden inspiration. On the other hand, modern critics have effected an adjustment of the old belief in his natural genius. At the least, he knew the Bible, in the Authorized and Geneva versions; John Foxe's *Book of Martyrs;* Martin Luther's *Commentary on Galatians;* the books of Dent and Bayley brought to him by his first wife; Samuel Clark's *A Mirrour and Looking-glass for both Saints and Sinners* and other such "judgment" literature; the "case of conscience" of Francis Spira; some "romances"; some works of George Herbert, Francis Quarles, and George Wither; Richard Bernard's *The Isle of Man;* and an inordinate amount of pamphlet and sermon literature of the period. He has borrowed from these works and sometimes quotes them directly or mentions them or their authors by name. However, Bunyan credited only Clark with a considerable number of direct contributions to his works; and he frequently stressed that his productions were his own, as in *Grace Abounding* and in the Advertisement to the Reader that is affixed to *The Holy War.*

The *real* Bunyan is also the stuff of legends. The major works reveal an expanding humanity that is dazzling in terms of his religious orientation. His wit and, above all, his zest for the myriad forms of mankind are constantly a surprise. They are present to a greater or lesser degree in *Grace Abounding,* Part I of *The Pilgrim's Progress, The Life and Death of Mr. Badman, The Holy War,* Part II of *The Pilgrim's Progress,* and *A Book for Boys and Girls.*

CHAPTER 2

Grace Abounding to the
Chief of Sinners

I *The Account*

BEFORE Bunyan recounts God's full mercies to him in his spiritual autobiography, *Grace Abounding to the Chief of Sinners* (1666), he gives a "hint" of his "low and inconsiderable genera-tion." Of a poor household, he was sent nonetheless to school and learned to read and write. As a child, he had few equals for cursing, swearing, lying, and blaspheming; but, even in childhood, God was "after him" with frightening dreams and visions. Greatly afraid of the Judgment, he often despaired of heaven at the early age of nine or ten. Eventually, these dreams left him, and he progressed to being the ringleader of vice among his friends. Even so, he was horrified to see evil in those who professed goodness. God's mercy remained with him, despite his evils; he was twice saved from drowning and was not poisoned when he once plucked the sting from an adder. Again, as he was about to leave for a siege, his place was taken by a soldier who was later shot in the head and killed.

Nothing changed Bunyan for the better, however, until he mar-ried a poor woman whose only dowry was Arthur Dent's *The Plaine Mans Pathway to Heaven* and Bishop Lewis Bayley's *The Practice of Piety*. These books along with stories about his wife's godly father attracted him to religion, and he attended church twice daily and "superstitiously" adored its trappings. He continued in this vein, worrying about whether he was a member of the chosen race of Israelites and never thinking about Christ, until a sermon on abuse of the Sabbath afflicted his conscience. He shook his mind of these spiritual worries soon enough until, one day in the

middle of a game of "tipcat," he heard a voice from heaven invit-
ing him to leave his sins.

Despairing that he was too late to avoid damnation, Bunyan
resolved to enjoy himself fully. But he was driven from swearing,
one of his great pleasures, by the rebuke of the most evil old
woman in the town; and he also became acquainted with and fell
under the influence of a man who "professed" religion. Turning to
the Bible, Bunyan made an outward reformation for about a year
and pridefully believed that his obedience to the Ten Command-
ments was pleasing to God. Bellringing and dancing were among
the most difficult to leave of his pleasures.

Bunyan's true spiritual insecurity was brought home to him at
last by an encounter with three or four poor women of Bedford
who were sitting in a doorway in the sun and talking about a "new
birth" and about the insufficiency of their own righteousness.
Moved by seeing this spiritual tableau, he doubted his purely
"moral" or "carnal" conversion. At this time, he also became
acquainted with a Ranter but was horrified by the extreme actions
of the man's sect. When Bunyan now renewed his search of Scripture, he particularly pondered the Pauline Epistles that he had formerly abhorred. He was obsessed with the question of whether he
had faith, and the Devil tempted him to test God through jumping
safely over "horse pads."

When the women of Bedford appeared to him in a vision, they
were separated from him by a wall whose gap he identified as Jesus.
He again questioned his election to salvation until a verse suddenly
came to him: "Look at the generations of old, and see, did ever any
trust in God and were confounded?" For over a year, he searched
for its source and found it at last in the Apocryphal Book of Ecclesiasticus. Again he thought about the tableau of the Bedford
women in the sun and despaired that he was too late to be saved
until a verse from Luke reminded him that there was "yet room" in
God's house. The women of Bedford also helped him by introduc-
ing him to their pastor, John Gifford.

Convinced that his only righteousness resided in Christ, Bunyan
feared inward pollution but was at length comforted by a sermon
on the Song of Solomon. But, alas, he was able to consider himself
Christ's "love" for fewer than forty days. He felt himself warned
of an approaching spiritual storm that settled on his soul and made
him question the authenticity and uniqueness of the Bible. During
the year of this tempest, he found his heart grow hard, while the

Devil tormented him with a desire to blaspheme. At last, he had a day memorable for its assurance. He again looked more closely into Scripture to perceive the perversities of the Quakers and the intricacies of the life of Christ. He longed for a written expression of an experience comparable to his, and he ultimately found it in Martin Luther's *Commentary on Galatians*.

He was assaulted for a year by the desire to exchange Christ for the things of this world, and he finally began to feel that he had "sold Christ" as Esau had sold his birthright. The despair of two years was broken by a Scriptural revelation that the blood of Christ remits all guilt; but, again despairing, Bunyan contrasted his selling of Christ with the cases of biblical figures who were saved because their sins were only against the Old Testament Law. Shamefacedly, he admitted that his spiritual companion was Judas; and his depression was intensified by the "case of conscience" of Francis Spira. Eventually, a great wind seemed to rush comfort to his soul, but he backslid after some three or four days. His great fear was that he could be saved only by Christ's coming again and that this return was impossible. He alternated between the security of grace and the desolation of having committed the "unpardonable sin" of selling Christ.

An apparent miracle during his wife's childbirthing quieted him until the next besetting temptation of atheism. He joined the Bedford congregation but was tempted to blaspheme the communion service. After the better part of a year, he suffered from consumption and from a worse bout of weakness in his inner or spiritual self. He was aroused from this lassitude by the knowledge that he was justified by grace, but he soon fell under another "cloud of darkness" from which he emerged into one of the best nights of his spiritual life.

Having been "awakened" to salvation through Christ for five or six years, Bunyan was invited to the ministry. He was at first reluctant to preach and would do so only in private; but he gradually reached the point that he would appear in public and before those who were not saved because the Scripture and John Foxe's *Book of Martyrs* had convinced him that one must not bury one's abilities. Still, he was not yet free from fear for the salvation of his soul, for his temptations freed him only at the church door and seized him again as he left the church. For two years, his sermons condemned the flesh by the Law; the next two years focused on Jesus; and approximately the next five years were spent on the mystery of and union with Christ, a period that culminated in a view of the minister's task as awakening and converting.

The Devil, unable to overthrow Bunyan's ministry with temptation, resorted to slander: accusations were rife that Bunyan was a witch, a Jesuit, a highwayman, and a profligate who kept whores, sired bastards, and had two wives. Bunyan forthrightly disavowed transgressions then or ever with women.

In prison, Bunyan worried about his ability to endure torture and to die well and about his family, especially blind Mary. He nevertheless felt a tremendous inpouring of Jesus; and his resolution never to deny his profession, a preacher of Christ, was a great comfort. In his conclusion, Bunyan admits, however, that he still suffers from seven temptations. Among them is his leaning to the works of the Law rather than to the spirit of Christ.

II *The Genre*

Grace Abounding belongs to the formal genre of "spiritual autobiography." While other works of this type, such as *The Confessions of Saint Augustine,* emphasize the spiritual life of the "confessor," *Grace Abounding* is remarkable for its lack of physical detail and therefore disappoints or at least surprises the seeker after facts. Though covering about thirty-two years of Bunyan's life, it offers a marked contrast to the autobiographical *A Relation of the Imprisonment of Mr. John Bunyan.* The grammar school Bunyan attended remains unidentified, Bunyan's wives are unnamed, but Esau and his birthright loom large. Any notations of time or concreteness of detail are associated only with the spiritual current of relief or despair. Thus Bunyan cannot "be delivered nor brought to peace again until well-nigh two years and an half were compleatly finished"[1] or "...about ten or eleven a Clock one day, as I was walking under a Hedge, full of sorrow and guilt God knows, and bemoaning myself for this hard hap ... suddenly this sentence bolted in upon me, *The Blood of Christ remits all guilt....*"[2] Spiritual time, not the minutia of daily life, is recounted.

Temporal and positional notices, reserved as they are for spiritual experiences, become the structural devices for assigning importance to this work as an account of inner growth. Yet, remarkably, great scenes leap from the pages, never to be forgotten: young Bunyan is interrupted during a game of "cat," just as he is about to strike his second blow, by a voice from heaven; the awestruck young man is condemned for his swearing by the notoriously evil old woman; Bunyan is mightily attracted to bellringing but is estranged from it by an apprehension of death from a falling bell or steeple; in a glorious vision, the Bedford women sit in the sun of God's grace. These scenes are simultaneously living ones for the reader and spiritual watersheds for Bunyan. The women in the sun, for example, act upon him just as the emblematic or symbolic pictures of the Interpreter's House act upon Christian and Christiana of *The Pilgrim's Progress.*[3] The artist-writer Bunyan almost unwittingly asserts his control, and he moves the materials of *Grace Abounding* beyond those of formal spiritual autobiography and mere "confession" alone.

Grace Abounding, written during Bunyan's first imprisonment, is also prison literature. Again, however, the reader feels that this genre is also incidental to the main intention of Bunyan; for the controlling parameter is the Puritan emphasis on the sharing of one's experience of regeneration, of conversion. In fact, relationships with the conversion process are implicit throughout *Grace Abounding.* Early in the work, Bunyan presents himself as instinctively hating the "fruitless professor" of religion who is so often condemned in the tinker's own writings and in other Nonconformist tracts. If Bunyan saw no action during his army career, the implication is that God somehow ordained the uniqueness of his life in this way. In the image popular among the sectaries, he was to be a "soldier of Christ." The influence of his first wife and her "dowry" sends him to church; Bunyan has passed through the first stage of the conventional Puritan conversion, conviction of sin, and is now in the second or "moral" phase. Here he indulges in a pharisaical fulfillment of the letter, rather than of the spirit, of biblical Law. Again, in a classic fashion, Bunyan alternately falls away from and is recalled to God. The throes of the despair he feels are those typically attendant upon moral conversion.

The event that is the turning point of Bunyan's spiritual life is the vision of the Bedford women sitting in the sun, a vision that is comparable to Paul's experience on the road to Damascus. It marks the distance between Bunyan's carnal reformation and his "rebirth" in Christ, for the women of Bedford make him understand the new birth of regeneration and the uselessness of good works without faith in the blood of Christ.

Bunyan's searching of the Scriptures is in compliance with the Nonconformist belief that personally applicable messages could be found therein. In particular, the Pauline Epistles to which he is drawn are the texts central to the Puritan doctrine of regeneration. And when he is comforted by the sermon on the Song of Solomon, Bunyan is reminding his audience of the standard Protestant interpretation of the Song of Songs as an allegory of Christ's wooing of a soul for God. Similarly, his admitting that he questioned the authenticity and uniqueness of the Bible is meant to remind the Puritan audience, who was taught to rely on Scripture for spiritual guidance and to believe in it literally, that the worst of sinners could be saved. In fact, the intensity of his trials establishes his credentials as a preacher in keeping with the Puritan belief that God tested the faithful now as He had tested Abraham and Job.

When Bunyan records his finding of Luther's *Commentary on Galatians,* he is able to substantiate the Puritan belief in the sharing of "cases of conscience," for he feels that he has found a situation comparable to his own. Like most of his fellow Puritans — and *for* them, here — Bunyan constantly plays off the Old Testament against the New, the true expression of Christ. He sees moral conversion as corresponding to the Old Testament; regeneration, to the New. Until the "old man" is weaned from the Law, the Old Testament, he cannot be regenerated by the spirit of Christ in the New. At the same time, a sin against the Law cannot be, as Bunyan points out to his audience, of the same magnitude as the unpardonable sin of denying Christ. Finally, implicit in Bunyan's tracing of his growth as a minister is a parallel with the movement of the standard pattern of Puritan conversion from life by the Law to life by the spirit of the Gospel in Christ.

Grace Abounding is Bunyan's most steadily serious major work. Its alternations of agonizing despair and of exultations (the "castings down and raisings up" of the preface) are the very pattern not only of the Old Testament rhythm of the chosen people, who fall away from and then are recalled to God, but also of human self-questioning, of the search for identity. Since Bunyan is concerned about establishing a working model of man's relationship with the deity, a duty incumbent upon Puritans generally, he consciously molded the narration of his experiences to delineate the standard Puritan pattern of conversion. Artistically and propagandistically shaped as the autobiography is, Bunyan's sincerity and agony remain unquestioned.[4]

Bunyan's (propagandistic) application of this conversion experience to others is demonstrated by his parenthetical "And I am very confident, that this temptation of the Devil is more than usual amongst poor creatures then many are aware of..."[5] and by his desire to share Christ's love even with the crows on the fence. At the same time, his "artistic" boast[6] that he is the "chief of sinners" whose crimes are greater than those of all the sinners against the Law combined, yea, "bigger than the sins of a Countrey, of a Kingdom, or of the whole World," is tempered by his repeated image of self-lowliness. He has, finally, one end in mind: the glorification of Christ. The more Bunyan boasts of his uniqueness as a sinner, the greater is Christ's bounty and the more hope there is for not-so-advanced sinners. His humble portrayal of himself also redounds praise to Christ: "...great Grace and small Gifts are better then great Gifts and no Grace."[7] Prison literature and spiritual autobiography Bunyan's *Grace Abounding* may be, but it is also, and principally, Puritan conscience-and-conversion literature that sings, artistically to be sure, the necessity for Christ.

III   *The Psychology*

Grace Abounding is a landscape of spiritual tableaux, as if somehow an electroencephalogram had been taken of this long-drawn-out soul crisis and as if the experimenter had then written discrete paragraphs translating each peak and valley. A book that is in many ways "psychological," it has been a favorite with psychologists and psychoanalysts. William James, for example, regarded Bunyan as a type of the "divided self," torn between the hostility of his actual and ideal selves.[8] Bunyan's difficulties in squeezing through the gap in the wall, in the vision of the Bedford women, have been interpreted as the archetypal birth egress image or as passage into an advanced religious state; and many have seen in this account similarities to modern anxieties and neuroses.

As a child, Bunyan suffered from terrible dreams of devils and of Judgment. Under later spiritual duress, he thought that he saw the Devil and felt Satan pull at his clothes. These sensations would have been the more horrible to a Puritan audience steeped in the right use of the faculties[9] as one of the approaches to God. Perhaps this belief in the data of the senses accounts for the wish fulfillment in Bunyan's looking over his shoulder to see if God is following with a pardon in His hand. Bunyan frequently feels that he is possessed by the Devil, and he sometimes cannot tell whether Satan or he himself speaks. Voices hold out comforts from Scripture or warnings of renewed temptations. Again, is it Satan or God who speaks to him?

Bunyan's descriptions are filled with images of torture, for his spiritual condition places him *on the wheel* and leaves him feeling as though he has *run upon pikes.* In a classic use of imagery, his fits of despair are storms, tempests, and winds that are mercifully followed by calms. At other times, clouds of darkness settle upon him, much in the manner of the mystic's "dark night of the soul"; and he uses the terminology of the mystic in describing himself as spiritually "thin." Psychosomatics are predominant: "I felt ... such a clogging and heat at my stomach by reason of this my terrour, that I was, especially at some times, as if my breast-bone would have split in sunder."[10] His very real bout of consumption is also attended by a sickness of his "inward man."

The most poignant psychological direction of his distemper, however, is represented by his longing for innocence and by his desiring to be anyone or anything but himself. When the old woman chides his swearing, he longs to be a child again. Afraid of being a reprobate, he wishes he were a creature, even a toad or a dog. And, in a moment of security, he wishes for death, as if he is certain that his peace will not last: "...O thought I, that I were fourscore years old now, that I might die quickly, that my soul might be gone to rest."[11] The Jobian hope of "dying in his nest" is never far from him.

The psychological import of *Grace Abounding* demonstrates that Bunyan is both a man of his religious milieu and an individual whose experience has universal application. The Puritans tended to map and chart the valleys and peaks, the exaltation and despair of the conversion experience until the sufferer took on the appearance of a modern-day manic-depressive. Very likely, this prescriptiveness forced upon some weaker souls, like those discussed in Robert Burton's *Anatomy of Melancholy,* a burden they were little able to endure. The stereotypic nature of the experience may have deprived others of intense feelings, but John Bunyan mastered the classic pattern *and* found its uniqueness. He managed to avoid in retelling the experience, as no doubt in living it, the florid emotional excesses of some of the groups on the Puritan left. He did not "speak in tongues" or "testify in the spirit," but true emotion is felt by Bunyan and by his audience. The Puritan emphasis on the right use of the faculties is much in evidence, for Bunyan exerts his reason and his will and ultimately makes the audience feel the self-mastery of his imagination.

IV The "People"

As intensely personal as the drama of Bunyan's soul is, one of the great points seems to be the positive or negative exemplary value of his contacts with people — a structured demonstration of the efficacy of his own work for others. Bunyan's implicit emphasis on personal relationships merges with the tendency of *Grace Abounding* to reduce physical detail to a minimum and to give full reality to the spiritual. Of his contemporaries, only John Gifford and a friend, one "Harry," whose story is retold in *The Life and Death of Mr. Badman* (1680), are named. His wife, his father, his godly father-in-law, the parson, an "ancient Christian," a "man who professed religion," and a friend who became a Ranter help Bunyan by example, by their conversations, or by their depictions of what not to do (for example, the so-called "heresies" of the Quakers send him on a more diligent search of Scripture).

Aside from these local figures and Martin Luther, Francis Spira, John Foxe, Arthur Dent, and Lewis Bayley, the other personages most real to Bunyan are biblical. Esau is especially important; but so are such figures as Saul, Judas, Manasseh, Peter, David, and Paul. Indeed, according to the preface, Bunyan derived from Paul part of his impetus for writing. However, one of the most amazing feats of *Grace Abounding* is its anthropomorphism of the Bible. Not only does Bunyan rise and fall emotionally with the pulse of particular biblical quotations, but the Bible itself becomes like a living being: "And as I was thus before the Lord, that Scripture fastned on my heart, *O man, great is thy Faith,* Matt. 15.28. even as if one had clapt me on the back...."[12] And the portion of Ecclesiasticus for which he has searched so long seems to *converse* with him. These aids, as he later comes to see, tend in one direction — to help Bunyan find Christ.

V Christ and the Retrospective Bunyan

The main character in *Grace Abounding* proves to be not Bunyan but Christ,[13] who has pursued this sinner by sending him dreams and by instilling in him a sense of horror at the hypocrisy of the allegedly righteous. The writer Bunyan views his religious experiences initially as a negation of Christ; during the "moral" phase of conversion, "...He never thought of him, nor whether there was one or no...."[14] Christ's mercy in keeping Bunyan alive on several occasions is brought home to him only retrospectively. It is, finally, the combination of the Pauline Epistles, to which Bunyan comes late, and the talk of conversion through Christ by such as the Bedford women that has set Bunyan after Christ as Christ has been shown to have sought out Bunyan.

The work becomes, in effect, another "holy war" between Christ and Satan for the prize of Bunyan's soul. The Christ-obsessed man feels that Satan is trying to tamper with his views of Christ. Bunyan's "unpardonable sin" is "selling Christ," and one of his most horrifying moments is his temptation to propose the relativity of religion: "Everyone doth think his own Religion right-est, both *Jews,* and *Moors,* and *Pagans;* and how if all our Faith, and Christ, and Scriptures, should be but a think-so too?"[15] The Devil finally uses Bunyan's obsession with Jesus to his own ends — Satan mimics Christ, and Bunyan is made to hear this Satan-Christ express pity for him but declare that he (as Christ) cannot return again to the world for the pleader.

The rational-writer Bunyan, looking back, recognizes his own foolishness: "These things may seem ridiculous to others, even as ridiculous as they were in themselves, but to me they were most tor-menting cogitations...."[16] This late-found rationality brought to a consideration of his former actions serves to intensify the reader's knowledge of the frenzy under which Bunyan has labored after Christ. When the reasoning Bunyan cannot make those experiences plausible, the effect is even more startling: "I have not yet in twenty years time been able to make a Judgment of it [the wind that comes upon him like a voice speaking]. *I thought then what here I should be loath to speak.*"[17]

Critics have recognized *Grace Abounding* as the product of the mature Bunyan who is looking back to interpret his preconversion and conversion lives, but they have not intimately connected his act of judging with the unfolding of *the* Christ-centered life. For exam-ple, John N. Morris considers the work's superior mark to be its analytic tone and judgment;[18] and Joan Webber distinguishes the Bunyan who experiences and the Bunyan who interprets.[19] Abun-dant evidence of Bunyan's judgment is present in the incidents he added to later editions (for example, the soldier who takes his place, his other escapes from danger, the bell-ringing episode, the

Ranter, Luther on Galatians, and the disavowal of the charges of
immorality). Most of these examples, however, give shape to the
same advancing Christ-consciousness that is outlined in his careful
delineation of the course taken by his preaching: from the Law, a
negation of Christ; to the life of Jesus; and to union with him.

VI *The Style*

As a result of its personal cast, *Grace Abounding* differs stylisti-
cally from Bunyan's other well-known works. The division into
paragraphs without a strong conventional narrative thread is rather
awkward, but this style is strangely effective for presenting a story
that is a series of moments of loss and triumphs. The proverbs that
tend to be plentiful in the remaining major works are generally
absent; Bunyan limits musical references to the ringing of the
church bells and to a comparison of the cymbal and its player to
gifts without grace; and his humor is absent, as is to be expected of
a work of this kind. The rhythms of his prose rise only through an
occasional use of alliteration and repetition: "...my Soul is dying,
my soul is damning";[20] the Tempter distracts him with a *bush, bull,*
and *besom* (a broom).[21]

In the preface, Bunyan maintains that his choice of style is deliberate: "...*God did not play in convincing of me; the Devil did not
play in tempting of me; neither did I play when I sunk as into a
bottomless pit ... wherefore I may not play in my relating of them,
but be plain and simple....*" Nevertheless, perhaps an unconscious pun creeps in with "...I began to sink greatly in my soul,
and began to entertain such discouragement in my heart, as laid me
low as Hell."[22] He does indulge slightly in his customary art of putting himself into a character and of endowing it with a unique
voice; thus Satan's "You are very hot for mercy, but I will cool
you...."[23] There are also some of the everyday comparisons, the
homely language for which Bunyan is noted: "By these things my
mind was now so turned, that it lay like a Horse-leach at the
vein...;[24] "...I have found my unbelief to set as it were the shoulder to the door to keep him out...";[25] and "...yea, my heart
would not be moved to mind that that was good, it began to be
careless, both of my Soul and Heaven; it would now continually
hang back both to, and in every duty, and was as a clog on the leg
of a Bird to hinder her from flying."[26] He may use familiar numbers to impress upon the reader the sincerity of his desire to mend:

"And now my heart was, at times, exceeding hard; if I would have given a thousand pounds for a tear, I could not shed one...."[27] "...Had I had a thousand gallons of blood within my veins, I could freely then have spilt it all at the command and feet of this my Lord and Saviour."[28]

Bunyan also attempts to convey his emotions through such exclamations as "But oh!" and "Alas, in vain"; through such physical states as "moping" into a field and "blushing" when he reads in Mark of the forgiveness of sins and blasphemies; and through comparisons and similes: he is "as those that jostle against the Rocks." Especially interesting among his similes are those that compare him to children, for he is like a child carried off by Gypsies or like a child who has fallen into a millpit. This ambiguity of desiring the child's innocence and of fearing its helplessness is another expression of his divided state of mind as he falls from safety into fear.

The same divisiveness results from his reading of Scripture. Some "blessed considerations" are made to "spangle" in his eyes; but, on the other hand, the Esau passage falls "like a hot thunderbolt" on his conscience. "O! one sentence of the Scripture did more afflict and terrify my mind ... than an Army of forty thousand men...."[29] "...but now a Word, a Word to lean a weary Soul upon, that I might not sink for ever!" he says, " 'twas that I hunted for."[30]

In addition to making the Bible a speaking character and allowing it to draw forth his emotional states, Bunyan demonstrates in *Grace Abounding* his expected skill in adapting it to his purposes. He takes Daniel's "weighed in the balance and found wanting" and converts it to a sustained dramatic portrayal of God's scales that weigh the texts on "sufficiency" and on Esau to determine whether Bunyan spiritually lives or dies. He is adept also at making biblical language express the change that comes over him when despair passes: "...with sweetness it returned upon me, as an ecco or sounding again, *I have loved thee with an everlasting love.*"[31]

Although *Grace Abounding* is approximately the thirteenth work from Bunyan's hand, he is still a virtual novice at the craft of writing as he was later to develop it. The spiritual autobiography is the first of his books to claim literary status, but already there are hints in it of the techniques he was to perfect. The experience of looking back to judge his past was no doubt a significant influence particularly on his emerging instinct toward the objectivity of allegory. Already, the ability to capture memorable moments reveals itself.

VII   *The Reluctance to Tell All*

The most unusual quality of *Grace Abounding,* especially since
Bunyan was, on one level at least, writing to help others, is his
reluctance to tell all. He is not simply pressed for time, as he com-
plains in the preface; nor is the cause only a desire for brevity:
"Many other things I might here make observation of, but I would
be brief..."[32]. There comes a point at which he deliberately seems
to insist that this experience is his and that each person must take
his or her own spiritual road. He suggests that a person who has so
closely touched heaven as he has through this experience *cannot* tell
all: "...at this time also I saw more in those words, *Heirs of God,*
Rom.8.17. than ever I shall be able to express while I live in this
world: *Heirs of God!* God himself is the portion of the Saints: this I
saw and wondered at, but cannot tell you what I saw"[33] and "...I
cannot now relate the matter as there I did experience it."[34]
   Through such reticence as "...I have also received, among
many things, much conviction, instruction, and understanding, of
which at large I shall not here discourse; onely give you, in a hint or
two, a word that may stir up the Godly to bless God, and to pray
for me; and also to take encouragement, should the case be their
own, *Not to fear what men can do unto them*"[35] and "Something
also there was upon my heart at the same time which I now cannot
call to minde...,"[36] Bunyan provokes in the reader a desire to find
out what is left unsaid; that is, to try Conversion Road for himself.
In effect, Bunyan accomplishes the aim he describes in the Apology
that prefaces Part I of *The Pilgrim's Progress:* "This Book will
make a Traveller of thee." In the Puritan tradition, he looks first to
his own spiritual state and then to others'; but the individual must
always take his own way. The refusal to tell all seems an artistic
device to provoke a spiritual response in the audience.
   The result is that *Grace Abounding* is both unique ("sincere")
and exemplary. Bunyan's own sense of its difference is best summarized by the way he distinguishes himself from his contemporaries: "...I did greatly long to see some ancient Godly man's
Experience, who had writ some hundred of years before I was
born; for, for those who had writ in our days, I thought (but I
desire them now to pardon me) that they had Writ only that which
others felt, or else had, thorow the strength of their Wits and Parts,
studied to answer such Objections as they perceived others were
perplexed with, without going down themselves into the deep."[37] In

this statement, Bunyan's parenthesis softens the note of the "chief of sinners" and reactivates the judging, reflecting writer who is looking back to see how he can make useful to others an experience that left him feeling as though the sun begrudged giving him light.

CHAPTER 3

Part I of
The Pilgrim's Progress

I *The Pilgrimage*

A S the narrator of Part I of *The Pilgrim's Progress* (1678), an allegory, walks through "the wilderness of this world," he comes upon a "den" or "jail" where he sleeps and dreams of a man in rags (later identified as "Christian"), who has a book in his hand and a burden on his back. This man's family believes that he is crazy, for he wanders through the fields asking what he can do to be saved. One by the name of "Evangelist" gives this man a parchment roll with instructions to fly the wrath to come and points the way to the Wicket-gate. The man, though unable to visualize the landmark, thinks he can see a shining light in that direction, sticks his fingers in his ears to avoid the calls of his family, and runs off crying after eternal life.

Two of his neighbors, Obstinate and Pliable, pursue him to bring him back; and Pliable is persuaded to accompany the man Christian, who reads about their anticipated rewards in a book. Their talk diverts their attention, and they fall into the Slough of Despond, an accident that is enough to convince Pliable to turn homeward. In spite of his burden, Christian struggles toward the farther side of the slough and is rescued by Help. When Christian then continues his journey, he meets Worldly Wise-man of Carnal Policy, who invites him to the village of Morality where he is to be received by Mr. Legality. To make this detour, Christian must pass a hill that flashes fire and threatens to fall on him. Again he is rescued, now by Evangelist, who admonishes him and directs him back to the way, the road he is traveling.

Christian soon arrives at a gate inscribed "Knock and it shall be opened to you"; and he is answered by Good-will, who quickly pulls him over the threshold lest he be struck by arrows from the castle of Beelzebub. Good-will, who shows Christian the "strait" (spiritually difficult) and narrow way, tells him that he will not be rid of his burden until he reaches the "place of deliverance." Christian's next stop is the House of the Interpreter, where he is shown a series of tableaux: the picture of a grave man; a dust-filled parlor; Passion and Patience; the Devil in the act of pouring water on a fire while Christ stands behind a wall feeding it with oil; a palace with a man taking names and a valiant man trying to fight his way to it; a man in an iron cage; and a man who has dreamed of Judgment. Having studied these emblems and having been sustained by their interpretations, Christian is anxious to leave; and he now finds the road fenced by the Wall of Salvation.

At the place of deliverance, the Cross, his burden falls off and rolls into a sepulcher below. Three shining ones dress him in new clothes, place a mark on his forehead, and give him a roll to present at the Celestial Gate. At the bottom of this hill of his deliverance, he finds Simple, Sloth, and Presumption in fetters. They are angry when he awakens them. Then Formalist and Hypocrisy leap the wall and argue that they have as much right as he to be now in the way to salvation, but they refuse to climb the Hill Difficulty; they take instead the byways of Danger and Destruction.

Midway to the top of this hill, Christian sleeps in an arbor and loses his roll. Hurrying to make up the lost time, he is passed by Timorous and Mistrust, who are fleeing in the opposite direction and who warn him of lions in the way. Christian is frightened; he seeks for his roll, then retraces his steps to the arbor. By the time he finds it and returns up the hill, night has come, and he must seek lodgings. In the distance, he spies the Palace Beautiful, but lions seem to block the way. The Porter Watchful calls to him that the animals are chained, and he hurries by to be invited in by Discretion and to discourse with Prudence, Charity, and Piety. After supper and more conversation, Christian is put to sleep in the Chamber Peace.

The next morning he is shown the rarities of the house: the pedigree of the Lord of the Hill, the records and "engines" of biblical heroes, and the armory. Then he is taken to the roof and shown the Delectable Mountains in the distance. He is armed, and the Porter informs him that Faithful, one of his former neighbors, has passed on the way. The damsels accompany him downhill, give him provisions, and warn him of the Valley of Humiliation. In this valley, Christian fights for his life the monster Apollyon, who tries to make him return to the service of the Devil. Ultimately, the giant flees; and a hand gives Christian some leaves from the Tree of Life to heal his wounds.

On his way once more, he meets two men who are fleeing in the opposite direction; and they warn him of satyrs, dragons, and hobgoblins. He proceeds, finding a ditch to his right and a quag to his left. The way is narrow and dark, and the mouth of hell emits sparks and noises. In this Valley of the Shadow of Death, Christian puts away his sword and takes out the weapon All-prayer. He suffers acutely, especially since demons make him think that he is blaspheming; but he is comforted first by a voice saying that he should fear no evil and then by the break of day. But the second part of the journey through this valley of death is even worse; the way is filled with traps, snares, and pits; and at its end are bones, ashes, and bodies, with a cave nearby that is inhabited by two frightful but now generally harmless giants, old Pope and (dead) Pagan.

Ascending from the valley, Christian sees Faithful ahead; but Faithful refuses to wait, and Christian runs past him. His pride trips him, however, and Faithful is able to join him. They talk of Faithful's encounters on the road with Wanton, Adam the first, Moses, Discontent, and Shame. Then they are joined by Talkative, and Faithful is impressed by the newcomer until Christian proceeds to enlighten his companion and to devise a method for being rid of this interloper. Affronted by their plain-dealing, Talkative departs; and they continue on their way, this time through a wilderness. When Faithful sees Evangelist walking behind them, they are informed by this figure that one of them will die in the town ahead.

The pilgrims arrive in the ancient market town of Vanity Fair. Their differences in dress and language cause a stir, especially since they put their fingers in their ears to avoid the attractions of the town's wares. They are ill-treated, and their good conduct wins some converts and enrages others of the townsmen. Eventually, they are brought to trial with Hate-good as judge, with three witnesses (Envy, Superstition, and Pickthank), and with a jury whose foreman is Blind-man. Although Faithful defends himself, he is found guilty and is then scourged, lanced, stoned, pricked with swords, and burned at the stake. But a chariot awaits him, and trumpets sound him to the Celestial Gate. Christian is imprisoned but manages to escape.

Hopeful now joins Christian in the journey, and they are met by By-ends, whom Christian recognizes even though he refuses to give his name. Unable to accept their terms of travel, By-ends falls in with Hold-the-world, Money-love, and Save-all; and these four discuss whether a man should feign religion to gain desired ends. When they decide to ask the opinion of Christian and Hopeful, they are confounded by Christian's negative response. Christian and Hopeful next pass over a delicate plain called Ease and come to the Hill Lucre with the silver mine of Demas. Hopeful is attracted, but Christian again prevents an error. By-ends and his materialistic friends, however, turn aside to Demas and are seen no more.

Christian and his companion find a new object of contemplation in the pillar of salt, and Hopeful ponders the difference between his sin and that of Lot's wife. Afterward, they spend the night on the banks of a river where grow trees with medicinal leaves and edible fruit, and they sing praises of the place. By this stage of the journey, their feet hurt, and Christian persuades Hopeful to climb a stile into By-path Meadow where they meet Vain-Confidence, who is shortly dashed to pieces by a fall into a pit. A storm befalls them; a voice warns that the way must be regained; and, heeding the warning, they are almost drowned and then decide to sleep until morning. But they have strayed into the grounds of the Giant Despair, who takes them to the dungeon of Doubting Castle and almost starves them. Diffidence, the giant's wife, persuades her husband to have them beaten and shown the bones of lost pilgrims in an effort to drive them to suicide. A death sentence is delivered, and Hopeful has to sustain the despairing Christian, who is remorseful because he has brought them to this pass. Suddenly, Christian remembers the key Promise that he has in his bosom; and they escape, stopping to engrave a warning on a pillar once they are over the stile again.

They travel on to the Delectable Mountains where they are entertained by the shepherds Knowledge, Experience, Watchful, and Sincere. The next morning, they walk on the mountains; and their hosts point out the hills of Error and of Caution, where men blinded by the Giant Despair are seen walking among tombs. They are also shown a door in a hill — the byway to hell. On the hill Clear, they try to look through the shepherds' perspective glass; but their hands shake so much that they cannot see the Celestial City.

They are sent on their journey with a note of the way and with warnings against the flatterer and against sleeping on the Enchanted Ground. As they speed on, the narrator wakes and sleeps to dream again.

Ignorance now climbs onto the way from the nearby town of Conceit. Christian maintains that this would-be pilgrim must enter by the gate; but Ignorance argues that his right living is sufficient for admission, and Christian and Hopeful pass him by. In a dark lane, Christian and Hopeful meet a wanton "professor" of religion whom seven devils have bound and are carrying back to the door in the side of the hill. Christian is prodded by this encounter to tell Hopeful the differences between Little-faith and Esau.

They travel on until one way runs into another so much that they cannot readily select the true path and are led astray by a flatterer, a man black of flesh but dressed in white, who suddenly throws a net over them. They remain enmeshed until a shining one frees them and chastises them with a whip, reminding them of the note of the way provided by the shepherds. They return to the road and go along singing when Atheist passes by heading away from Sion. Hopeful desires to rest in the Enchanted Ground; but, when Christian remembers their warning, they go along, talking to prevent sleep. Hopeful gives a long account of how he became a pilgrim. When Ignorance joins them again, the conversation turns to justification through Christ; but, not being pleased with the overtones, Ignorance, who really prefers to travel alone, falls behind. Hopeful and Christian continue to talk, this time of right fear and of backsliding.

Finally, when they arrive at the beautiful country of Beulah, Christian falls sick of desire for the Master (Christ). Two men approach them with a warning of their last difficulties. They begin to cross the River of Death, whose depth depends upon one's faith. Christian desponds and suffers from apparitions of hobgoblins and evil spirits. He eventually is able to renew hope, and both cross to leave their mortal garments behind and to be helped up a steep hill. The saints await them; and they learn that they will ride in chariots, help with the Judgment, and partake of the Marriage Supper of the Lamb (Christ). The King's trumpeters greet them with a melodious noise; the city's bells ring; and they receive certificates, harps, and crowns. The gates of the Celestial City close behind them, and the narrator wishes himself among them. He turns to see Ignorance being ferried over the river by Vain-hope. Ignorance knocks but can show no certificate; the two shining ones who conducted Hopeful and Christian to the city bind him; and then they fly with him to the door in the side of the hill. The narrator thus learns that there is a way to hell even from the gates of heaven, and he awakens to discover that he has been dreaming.

II *The Meaning of the Allegory*

Part I of *The Pilgrim's Progress* allegorizes the personal experience of conversion that Bunyan had presented in *Grace Abounding*. Dante's "Wood of Error" in the *Divine Comedy* becomes for Bunyan, the narrator, the "wilderness of this world." The "den" or "jail" represents Bunyan's own imprisonment, for he is believed to have started writing this work during the latter part of his first incarceration; it also symbolizes the predicament of man — imprisoned in the flesh unless he is reborn in Christ.

Christian, the protagonist, with his book and his burden, has searched the Bible and knows of his part in Original Sin. The lengthy process by which Bunyan, in *Grace Abounding,* arrived at the first stage of conversion, conviction of sin, is greatly curtailed for Christian. The answer to his question of what such a sinner can do to be saved comes from a "preacher of good tidings," Evangelist, who is like Bunyan's own John Gifford and who directs Christian to the Wicket-gate or Christ's grace. When Christian flees his family and seeks eternal life, Bunyan is presenting the emergence of faith and the first act of turning one's back on the things of this world.

Throughout the work, the Puritan emphasis on that infallible guide, the Bible, is maintained: Christian reads it to learn of the reward of eternal life. Bunyan implies that a close study of the Bible would also prepare him for bouts of despair, as biblical rhythms delineate the falling away from and the being recalled to God of religious seekers. The Slough of Despond stresses such an onset of despair and the fact that help will be forthcoming to spiritual pilgrims who refuse to be paralyzed by it.

Like Bunyan in *Grace Abounding,* Christian must learn, in this journey toward Christ and eternal life, to exchange the good works of the "moral" stage of conversion for the faith in Christ of subsequent stages. To make him aware of this contrast, Bunyan introduces him to Worldly Wise-man, Mr. Legality, and the village of Morality. The frights associated with this detour into the "world" present the terrors attendant upon the legalism of the Old Testament. All Christians, present in Christian, must shun the world, be vigilant and active, and contemplate spiritual matters, as Christian becomes contemplative in the House of the Interpreter.

From Bunyan's point of view, however, the most significant event of the pilgrimage occurs at the Cross, where Christian loses his burden. Here is Christ's substitution of himself as payment for the Original Sin of man. Christian has now been *called* to salvation and is *justified* by his faith in Christ. His "rags," symbolizing the Old Man or Old Adam, are replaced by the new clothes that betoken his being "born again" in Christ. Nonetheless, Christian cannot rest on his laurels; the conversion process involves constant vigilance. Christian sleeps and loses his roll and becomes, momentarily, a backslider. He is allowed to compensate for this failure, however, by asserting the faith that carries him beyond the lions. Since he must also be vigilant of mind, these physical adventures are followed by another bout of mental activity in the House Beautiful. Here, in this place for contemplation, he symbolizes the intertwining of sapience and fortitude necessary to the pilgrim as he is "armed" and becomes the true "wayfaring, *war*faring" Christian. Lest he become prideful in his new guise, however, he is next tested in the Valley of Humiliation and in the Valley of the Shadow of Death to remind him of the ignominiousness of Christ's experience and of the necessity for constant revaluation of his religious commitment. In the second valley, he suffers acutely and, like Bunyan in *Grace Abounding,* is beset by demons who make him think that he is blaspheming or "selling Christ."

Faithful and Hopeful unfold alternative ways of traveling to heaven, and Bunyan also emphasizes through them the efficacy of shared experiences among the brethren. By the same token, false pilgrims like Ignorance and By-ends warn Christian and the audience against employing wrong ways of worship. By-ends, in particular, is Bunyan's critique on all those who have tried to use shortcuts and byways to achieve heaven. Ignorance is guilty of believing that man can earn salvation by good works, and the implication is that Christ's sacrifice was unnecessary. Ignorance is also ignorant of the mutual benefits of the society of believers stressed by the Puritans. Overconfidence and diffidence were other besetting problems of the Puritans, and Bunyan juxtaposes them as he underscores Christian's failures through Vain-Confidence and then introduces (in a later edition of the work) Diffidence, the wife of Despair.

Over and over comes the message that the pilgrim can never be absolutely confident of salvation; he must constantly work toward that end. Thus Christian, with Faithful, is again reminded of the evils of the world in Vanity Fair; for Bunyan satirizes through it the ways of the world, reveals its treatment of the faithful, and examines martyrdom. Late in their journey, Christian and Hopeful again fail in vigilance as they fall prey to the flatterer.

Bunyan's message is a harsh one. Not even total vigilance will carry the pilgrim to heaven. Rather, on the hill Clear, Christian and Hopeful must take on *faith* alone that they can see the Celestial City through the shepherds' perspective glass. Faith must convey them onward as it has formerly turned Christian toward the Wicket-gate and Bunyan toward the women of Bedford who were separated from him by a wall. Indeed, at the last instant, Christian suffers a failure of faith that he can be saved. Crossing the River of Death, with the heavenly city before him, he despairs and feels that he is drowning. Though he becomes more and more centered on Christ and Christ's saving power, the pilgrim can still experience crises of the soul. Bunyan's spiritual realities are stern. Interestingly, however, it is not death itself that is frightening for the pilgrim; it is only the lapses of faith in being saved.

The emphasis on faith is, in fact, underscored artistically in *The Pilgrim's Progress,* Part I. The narrator awakens (and then sleeps to dream again) at the point in the narrative where Christian and Hopeful take *on faith* that they can see heaven through the perspective glass. In personal terms, Bunyan has thus signaled an interruption of the work as the first imprisonment came to an end and a return to it with the onset of the shorter second prison term. When Christian, at the end, overcomes his lack of faith, crosses the river (dies), and enters heaven, the narrator again reacts to a situation centered on faith. He wishes to be in heaven, too. Bunyan implies, however, that one must not seek martyrdom, but must, *in faith,* wait on God's time to reach heaven. Ironically, it is *Faithful* who has been martyred in Vanity Fair. Only God could decide, finally, whose persecution, like that of Bunyan's prison days, would end with the martyr's palm of victory.

III *Its "Chameleonism" and Its Genre(s)*

An undergraduate philosophy and religion major remarked during a class discussion of Bunyan that Part I of *The Pilgrim's Prog-*

ress was the most pleasant account of death he had ever read. But one of the problems the teacher faces is that today's students are apt to read the work without realizing that it is about death, for they tend to associate Christian with the heroes of folk and fairy tradition and with chivalric romance. Accordingly, they expect him to win through his *athlon* (or struggle) to victory; and they are not easily convinced that the rewards of a certificate, a crown, and a harp fit the story.

Perhaps after all, this view is not a problem but a testimony to the chameleon quality of the work that Roger Sharrock regards as a hybrid of religious allegory, the early novel, the moral dialogue, the romance, and the folk story.[1] He might have added to that list, as other critics have, the picaresque novel, the epic, the dream-vision, and the fairy tale. This narrative has also been labeled a social document, a Calvinist tract, and a child's story. In fact, Daniel Defoe's *Robinson Crusoe,* Lewis Carroll's *Alice in Wonderland,* and even L. Frank Baum's *The Wizard of Oz* are among the more popular novels that students tend to cite as parallels; and Guillaume de Deguileville's *Pelerinage de la vie humaine (The Pilgrimage of the Human Life)*, William Langland's *Piers Plowman,* Richard Bernard's *The Isle of Man,* Edmund Spenser's *The Faerie Queene,* Homer's *Odyssey,* and medieval and Puritan sermon literature are among the favorite source haunts.

Most critics interested in allegory approach *The Pilgrim's Progress* with some dismay, since they are usually forced to recognize that it contains not only allegorical but realistic and psychological components, among others. Some finally insist that it is not allegorical but parabolic,[2] and J. W. Mackail finds Bunyan elusive about his intention: "The words he uses himself in speaking of it are many and various: metaphor, parable, figure, shadow, similitude, fable, romance; but he keeps falling back on the word dream [*sic*] as what comes nearest to the truth."[3] As *The Pilgrim's Progress* was probably written with little awareness of the literary tradition behind it, Bunyan was certain to take liberties with the genre; and perhaps H. E. Greene is correct in his view that this work is so perfect because it is not perfect allegory.[4]

There is general agreement that what makes *The Pilgrim's Progress* succeed is the input of realism; for the characters, by an endowed trait or a turn of speech, leave the old allegorical realms of personified vices and virtues and function as individuals as well as types. In fact, it is now common practice to suggest historical

persons as models for the characters — Edward Fowler, the Latitudinarian Anglican, as By-ends; John Gifford, as Evangelist; Mercy,
as "Mary" Bunyan, the first wife; Christiana, of Part II, as Elizabeth, the second wife — and to offer Bunyan's use of models as one
reason for his realistic character portrayal. Likewise, the area of
Elstow and Bedford has been searched for particular topographical
details of the journey; and it is fashionable to point out Bunyan's
maplike precision of contours, even though, when he turns from
features that do not show the regularity and flatness of Bedfordshire, he tends to be somewhat vague of description.

A high mark of *The Pilgrim's Progress* as a realistic work is Bunyan's refusal to fall into the trap of painting moral absolutes,
whether of places or of men. Hills, for example, are not always
righteous: balancing Sinai, the place with the Cross, and the Delectable Mountains are Lucre, Error, and Caution. And, as in *Grace
Abounding,* evil places and people may help by performing as
negative exemplars. Most often, Bunyan's technique is to have
landscapes produce effects consonant with the viewer; for, as many
have suggested, the experiences at various points of the journey
correspond to the inner state of the pilgrim. The classic example is
the Valley of Humiliation, which is so frightful for Christian but so
suitable for Mr. Fearing of Part II. Generally, critics are agreed
that, with the exception of Ignorance,[5] Bunyan is inordinately fair
to his "bad" characters. Christian blushes for shame when Evangelist has to return to help him, but Talkative and Demas also blush
and prove thereby that they cannot be wholly despicable.

The *true* pilgrims also display the mixed nature of the human and
frequently evoke a sense of the comic as they reveal their frailties.
The audience responds with sympathy and mild laughter when
Talkative is "outtalked" by Christian and Faithful and is amusingly confounded by Christian's revelation that there is "knowledge, and knowledge." Christian suggests that he and Hopeful turn
out of the way into By-path Meadow because, quite understand-
ably, their feet hurt; even those on the road to salvation suffer the
foibles of human frailty. After he has seen several "significant"
sights at the Interpreter's House, Christian is impatient, as normal
people would be, to get on the road and to prove himself; and he is
restrained only by the efforts of his teacher.[6] Again, Christian
cannot resist a proud smile when he overruns Faithful; and Bunyan
cannot resist giving him his comeuppance. Both Faithful and Christian secretly long to be the martyr of Vanity Fair, a battle of pride

Bunyan himself must have fought early in his career. Hopeful is piqued when his companion "snibbeth" him (a term in the margin, but excised after the first edition). Worldly Wise-man tells Christian to heed him as older and wiser; and the pilgrim's mistake here comes again to haunt him when Hopeful says that he followed, as he was taught, the advice of his elders and so ended up in the hands of the Giant Despair. Later editions, though they excise some of Bunyan's marginal comments, add rich and often comic detail to the portraits of the minor characters. The objectivity of allegory seems to have encouraged Bunyan's wit, and it is perhaps true that "English comedy lost a master when Bunyan was born Puritan."[7] At any rate, Bunyan attains a unique blending of comedy and realism, for example, in Pliable's reception upon returning home and in the fact that Faithful does not recognize Talkative as a fellow townsman because the Town of Destruction is so large!

But Part I of *The Pilgrim's Progress* is primarily a religious work. As Maurice Hussey has indicated, Christian is not really Everyone but one of the elect.[8] At the beginning, he is convinced of his sin; and, like Bunyan in *Grace Abounding,* he wants desperately to be saved. The remarkable structural achievement, if his case is compared with Bunyan's, is how early in the way he recognizes the necessity for justification by Christ and so loses his burden of Original Sin. Christian never seems to face the abject soul-terror of Bunyan, not in the deepest passages of his despair; but he experiences the same current of alternating jubilation and casting down of the spirit. It is almost as if, once past the place of the Cross, Christian is troubled by the lesser fits and starts of Bunyan after he became a preacher.

This less intense conversion of Christian may result from its diffusion among various characters, although the intensity that must be sacrificed is compensated for by Bunyan's emphasis on the individuality of the soul's journey. Like Bunyan, Christian is greatly influenced by a preacher, Evangelist. But the stage of moral conversion is demonstrated not so much by Christian as by Formalist, Talkative, By-ends, and, particularly, Ignorance; for, like Bunyan in *Grace Abounding,* they think that nothing can be more pleasing to God than their compliance with the Law and their substitution of good works for faith. The right approaches to pilgrimage are shared by Christian, Faithful, and Hopeful; and Bunyan defines the differences between the spiritual qualities of the last two in *Israel's Hope Encouraged* (first printed in 1692). By having Hopeful spring from the ashes of Faithful, Bunyan also underscores the mutual dependence of believers that is presented in the Palace Beautiful and in the talk of Hopeful and Christian as they cross the Enchanted Ground. If those who gain heaven become more varied (a foreshadowing of Part II), they perhaps also become more applicable to their varied audience.

Using the two great traditional themes of life as a pilgrimage and of the necessity for being a wayfaring/warfaring Christian battling for the soul, Bunyan yet adapts these to his personal sense of the way to Christ. Christian is "*Grace*-less" unless he tries to find Christ; for, though Christ died for all, only those who respond to that grace will be saved. And both Bunyan and Christian suffer the fear that they are predestined to be among the damned. The hardest battle for many of the characters and for many Puritans is their prostrating themselves by admission of their own worthlessness and their recognizing that righteousness is only in Christ.[9] As with *Grace Abounding*, the real hero of this work may be Christ.

IV   *The Use of Scripture*

The religious theme of *The Pilgrim's Progress* is reinforced by Bunyan's marginal notations; but, as in *The Holy War* (1682), the Bible is seldom so obtrusive as it is in the piling up of biblical quotations in *The Life and Death of Mr. Badman* (1680). Young readers are likely to interpret the "strait and narrow way" and Christian's "girding up his loins" proverbially rather than Scripturally.[10] Christian's leaps of joy may be taken naturalistically rather than in association with the prefiguring, in the Old Testament, of Christ's coming "leaping among the hills" that is used by Bunyan in *The Holy War* when Emmanuel learns that mankind needs help. God himself is presented as the "governor of the country," and Christian is treated to the *pedigree* of "the Lord of the Hill." The fourth shepherd's bidding Christian and Hopeful "God speed" becomes a quibble. One may likewise skim over the way's being fenced by the Wall of Salvation without pondering its biblical significance. The use of the Bible is reinforced only at odd moments when Bunyan feels that he has not welded in his spiritual backdrop carefully enough. Thus he is forced to intrude into one of the sentences of Christian's self-recriminations for losing his pardon or roll: "(Thus it happened to *Israel* for their sin, they were sent back again by the way of the Red-Sea)."[11] These lapses are occasional only, as when he stops to give Christian's former name and to identify him as "of the race of Japhet" or to put a biblical inscription over the Wicket-gate.

Generally, the integration of the Bible into the text is consonant with the simultaneous manipulation of different levels or interpretations of the whole pilgrimage; and Bunyan should be more closely studied for his approach to the typology so often practiced in seventeenth-century theology. The biblical story of Hagar is updated by Bunyan's providing her with the son Legality, as he once more counterpoints the contrast between the legality of the Old Testament and the spirituality of the New. The stir caused by the "strange" language and behavior of Christian and Faithful in Vanity Fair might be a satire of the human's inability to accept that which is different from him, as well as a dramatization of Ecclesiastes' "vanity of vanities," until, of course, Bunyan identifies the new language as that of Canaan, a technique that he also applies to Christiana in the opening of Part II. Again, Hopeful's account of his conversion uses the analogy of the "old debt." This phrase is a metaphor for Original Sin and picks up the monetary language of Bunyan's day, which he often associated with the Devil, for example, in Apollyon's preliminary offer to raise Christian's wages, as well as in *The Life and Death of Mr. Badman* and *The Holy War*. The blending of different levels of interpretation is well exemplified also by Faithful's paralleling of Talkative with Moses' description of clean and unclean beasts, applied earlier in *Grace Abounding,* and by the display of biblical figures who use religion as a "stalking horse" — among them, Hamor and Shechem, whose story reappears in a similar context in *Badman*.

In keeping with the millenarian cast of Bunyan's period, the backdrop for the story is primarily Revelation, which was already so informative for *The Holy City* (1665), and the Song of Songs. These are at once large and localized influences. The final stage of conversion, glorification, takes place only after death and is symbolized in *The Pilgrim's Progress* by the crossing of the river. Both Revelation and the Song of Solomon contain promises of the faithful's union with Christ after the arduous journey to the Celestial City. Specifically, Revelation is the source for the changing of Pilgrim's clothes and for the mark of the redeemed in his forehead, with Apollyon and Wanton as forms of Antichrist and the Great Whore of Babylon, respectively. The most outstanding use of Canticles is in the description of Beulah, which means "married";

and Christian's being "sick of [from] love" necessitates knowledge that Canticles, like Revelation, was interpreted, among other ways, as the marriage of Christ and his Church or of Christ and the elect. Accordingly, the meals in the House Beautiful and with the shepherds symbolize not only the Christian fellowship that is touted by Christian and Hopeful but unappreciated by Ignorance, the dominant Old Testament theme of hospitality, the Last Supper, and the "love" feasts of the New Testament,[12] but also the celebration of the union of God and man in the Marriage Feast of Christ.

The Pilgrim's Progress can be read without a full knowledge of Revelation and the Song of Songs; but, by emphasizing both Christian's need to be responsive to the Bible and the spiritual effort he must constantly exert, Bunyan seems to remind the Puritan reader of its preeminent authority. Though Christian's is a much more active journey than that of his family in Part II, he also must participate in *mind*-work, as in understanding the emblems presented in the House of the Interpreter.[13] An impressive example of an emblemlike use of the Bible for personal education occurs when the pilgrims pause at the pillar of salt, which anticipates the many monuments of Part II. The discourse on the difference between Hopeful and Lot's wife is salutary in itself, but the ramifications for Christian's leaving behind of his family are far more important.

Bunyan has often been blamed for a *faux pas* here — even Huck Finn was struck by it — and Christian's fleeing with his fingers in his ears is taken, along with the treatment of Ignorance, as an example of the sterner and more Calvinistic tone of Part I. But Christian's and Lot's concern for their wives would have served them far worse than Orpheus was served by looking back at Eurydice. One of Bunyan's great themes was, always, that the human must give up this world for Christ, however painful that loss might be in the case of one's family. Ignorance does not forego the world; Christian does and so did Lot. Bunyan's humanity resides in the fact that he knew what such abnegation could cost. In *The Heavenly Foot-man* (1698), he ponders Lot's being able to resist turning to his wife, but he cites her as a negative example of the runner for Heaven: "How was *Lot's* Wife served for Running *lazily,* and for giving but one *look behind* her, after the things she left in Sodom?"[14] In Part I, the episode of the pillar of salt explains Bunyan's point of view to the reader and exercises the minds of Christian and Hopeful, providing at the same time a change of pace from the adventures of the road. Perhaps its most amazing feature, however, is the interpenetration of Scripture in the lives of the characters.

V   *Language and Style*

Bunyan is known for his colloquial style, which here masterfully undermines the distancing associated with the formal genre of allegory. The language is that of seventeenth-century village life. Christian's family is sure that he suffers from a "frenzy distemper." Christian describes himself as "musing in the midst of my *dumps*" when Evangelist comes a second time to his rescue, and he is almost "pressed to death" by Apollyon. Talkative talks the same on the "alebench" as on the road to salvation, and the Giant Despair pursues Christian and Hopeful with a good "crab tree cudgel." Abraham, Isaac, and the other saints are not simply floating on clouds or walking the streets of Heaven; they are "now resting upon their Beds." The exclamations of the characters smack of those of Restoration dandies, as in Obstinate's "tush" and Christian's summons of Faithful with "Ho, ho, So-ho" just prior to his vainglorious surge beyond that pilgrim. Bunyan's rural distrust of townsmen is perhaps activated in such moments, for usually those who mimic the language of the town stand in need of correction.

The false pilgrims who prance and posture as would-be gentlemen are earthbound men who believe in only what they can see. Demas and Worldly Wise-man are both gentlemen, as is that "old gentleman" Legality; and the true pilgrims are prone to succumb to their geniality and hauteur. Thus Christian's excuse for heeding Wise-man is that "He looked like a Gentleman...." By-ends makes "a very low *Conje*," or bow, typical of the behavior of the Diabolonians in *The Holy War*. And, though By-ends is forced to admit that there is a waterman in his ancestry and that he himself is indeed a waterman, he discourses on his genealogy. He exults over the fact that his wife, the daughter of Lady Faining, is "arrived to such a pitch of Breeding" and delights in his refined religion: "...First, we never strive against Wind and Tide. Secondly, we are always most zealous when Religion goes in his Silver Slippers...."[15] Bunyan is, of course, criticizing the decorum of the Anglicans; but he must also have simply enjoyed putting his characters to strutting.

Many of these false pilgrims have a facility for language that sounds well but says nothing, as Bunyan emphasizes with "Mr.

Say-well of Prating-row." Talkative is the perfect conversationalist: ". . . I will talk of things heavenly, or things earthly; things Moral, or things Evangelical; things Sacred, or things Prophane; things past, or things to come; things forraign, or things at home; things more Essential, or things Circumstantial. . . ."[16] Still others talk the language of practicality; the "gate-crashers" Formalist and Hypocrisy are on the road and that is that: "if we are in, we are in."

Among the wholesome sprinkling of proverbs are "a bird in the hand" and the dog who returns to its vomit, apparently a favorite with Bunyan and used twice in Part I. Puns or quibbles are more in evidence than usual. Christian rebukes sleep, for whose sake he is "like to be benighted" (caught by darkness; be damned). Faithful recalls the "heat" (emotional pitch; token of their being damned to hell) of the discourse of those in the City of Destruction. "You did well to talk so plainly to him [Talkative] as you did; there is but little of this faithful dealing with men now a days. . . ,"[17] Christian tells Faithful and scores a triple pun with "faithful" (Faithful; true-to-the-mark or plain; in a manner becoming a faithful man). Less clever is Christian's "But *Little-Faith,* though it was his lot to have but a *little faith,* was by his *little faith* kept from such extravagancies. . . ."[18] The lock of the iron gate of Doubting Castle goes *"damnable* hard," a play on words that greatly disturbed early editors; but they do not seem to have been bothered by a similar one, *"damnable Apostate,"* on the back of the man carried off to hell by the seven devils.[19]

As Bunyan indicates in the preface to the continuation, his *The Pilgrim's Progress,* Part I, pleased men, women, and children and was even popular in other countries, though some of his fellow Baptists had chastised it for being a "romance." At least part of the explanation for its success resides in the fact that Bunyan makes of it almost a game, albeit a serious one. Riddle-solving is, for Bunyan, another name for reading Scripture and for responding properly to *The Pilgrim's Progress,* Part I. Riddles, of which he was always fond, are for the most part confined to the outline of intention in the preface — "Would'st thou read Riddles, and their Explanation, / Or else be drownded in thy Contemplation?" — and to some of the adaptations of emblems in the House of the Interpreter. The title pages of both parts cite Hosea 12:10, "I have used similitudes"; and Bunyan defends his use of "metaphors" on the grounds that the Bible uses them, along with "dark figures," "types," "shadows," and "allegories." These and other terms fill the Author's Apology of Part I and help to summarize his work as "Truth within a Fable," so that, while some of his serious friends may have opposed its publication, he believes that "Dark Clouds bring Waters."

For all of its doctrine and its riddlelike qualities, Part I is a work of art whose author sought variety and change of pace. By the device of alternating body- and mind-work, Bunyan throws into relief the dangers of physical and mental inactivity — not only in the episode of Christian's losing his roll, but in the very name of the porter of the Palace Beautiful, *Watchful,* and in the humor created when Timorous and Mistrust flee *chained* lions. Then Bunyan presents the great episodes that have captured the hearts of painters and engravers as well as readers: Evangelist's pointing the way, memorable in William Blake's treatment; Christian's running from his home with his fingers stuck in his ears; the starkness of the place of the Cross versus the bustle of Vanity Fair, where British Row, French Row, and so on recall Shakespeare's fondness for satirizing national types; and the trial itself, which, despite its humorous and wonderful ticket-names, is so circumstantial that Bunyan must have been recalling his own presence before the bar. The narrator's dream and his obtruding into the narrative provide not only variety but a haunting, almost archetypal quality that is missed in the more circumspect dreamer of Part II.

Other aspects add to the artistry of the narrative. There are dreams-within-the-dream, such as the man who dreams of Judgment or Christian's and Hopeful's talking in their sleep; but no episode has the full poignancy of the narrator's wistful death wish as the gate closes behind Christian and Hopeful. Interest is heightened as well by the periodic arrivals of intermeddlers who clamber over walls and glide forth from byways; by tests of physical courage (Apollyon, Vanity Fair); by tests of faith (the river); and by tests of perception (the lions in the way). Bunyan may also use jog-trot verse to close episodes or to indicate their significance. But Christian's verse commemoration of Faithful is not so effective as the near-lyrical prose Bunyan uses to describe, in terms of the phoenix legend, the emerging of Hopeful from the ashes of Faithful. Autobiographical and religious, *The Pilgrim's Progress,* Part I, is also literary; and Bunyan's deliberate choice of an art form for this work suggests that he was becoming gradually conscious of his powers as a writer.

VI *Standard Bunyanesque Themes*

Already, as is the case with technique, Bunyan shows a constancy in his choice of minor materials and themes outside the main concerns with life as a pilgrimage and with conversion. Always insistent upon vigilance, for example, he usually offers at least a glance at the religion which had at one time been a serious menace. By his criticisms of the Catholics, he not only cautions against overconfidence but makes his audience retrace the history of the church, one of the great themes of *The Holy War.* In *The Pilgrim's Progress,* Part I, there is a humorous portrait of "Pope": "...though he be yet alive, he is by reason of age, and also of the many shrewd brushes that he met with in his younger dayes, grown so crazy and stiff in his joynts, that he can now do little more then sit in his Caves mouth, grinning at Pilgrims as they go by, and biting his nails, because he cannot come at them."[20] A reference is also made to the "Ware of *Rome*" offered at Vanity Fair.

More persistent and more closely related to the major theme of conversion is the stressing of the right use of the faculties. Though music is at a minimum (the trumpets at the chariot of Faithful and in the Celestial City or an occasional song by the travelers), the aural sense and the faculties in general receive the expected Bunyanesque and standard Puritan emphasis. Right use of the faculties is related to truth in the Author's Apology and becomes a justification for the "style" of Part I:

> *Come, Truth, although in Swadling-clouts, I find*
> *Informs the Judgement, rectifies the Mind,*
> *Pleases the Understanding, makes the Will*
> *Submit; the Memory too it doth fill*
> *With what doth our Imagination please....*

Like *Grace Abounding,* this work lays heavy stress on memory, which is a part of the mind-work of the pilgrims. Remembering Scripture, Christ, and past experience is an obligation of the current pilgrim to himself and to others who read or hear of his conversion.[21] This Puritan emphasis on memory helps to explain both that abrupt and humorous moment when Christian recalls the key of Promise and the frequent misadventures resulting from failure to remember the "note of the way" or the warning against the flatterer.

Like other Puritans, Bunyan gave preeminence to the aural sense, particularly in *The Holy War,* and secondary importance to the visual. No reader forgets the use of these senses in the opening of Part I of *The Pilgrim's Progress.* Evangelist tries to get Christian to *see* the Wicket-gate (Christ); when his effort fails, he points out a light in the same direction, and Christian "thinks" he can see it. Then Christian blocks the calls of his family and friends (the world) by placing his fingers in his ears. He thus activates the *eye of faith* in the first instance and the *ear of faith* in the second. The latter act is repeated (*remembered?*) by Christian and Faithful in Vanity Fair when they close their ears to its lures.

It is poetically fitting that heaven comes to Christian and Hopeful first through these same two senses: "...And now were these two men, as 'twere, in Heaven, before they came at it; being swallowed up with the sight of Angels, and with hearing of their melodious notes. Here also they had the City it self in view, and they thought they heard all the Bells therein to ring, to welcome them thereto: but above all, the warm and joyful thoughts that they had about their own dwelling there, with such company, and that for ever and ever."[22] On their way there, the inhabitants of the Interpreter's House and the Palace Beautiful have nourished their sight. Even with the shepherds, however, when they are close enough to heaven to view it through a perspective glass, the human veil is too great; and they can only sense through faith what mortal eyes cannot see. The aural sense is nurtured by the frequent warnings of such good-wishers as Prudence, Charity, Piety, Discretion, and the shepherds; but these warnings, again because of human frailty, are of no avail. Knowing Christian's vulnerability to the aural sense, Satan tries to terrify him by voices and horrible cries in the Valley of the Shadow of Death. Through these references to the faculties, Bunyan champions individual responsibility. The faculties can lead to God and were meant as an aid to man; perverted, as in the charge that Formalist and Hypocrisy "walk by the rude working of their fancies," they lead only into the world and, like the byways throughout the work, thus lead nowhere.

CHAPTER 4

The Life and Death of
Mr. Badman

I *The Story*

The Life and Death of Mr. Badman (1680) is a dialogue between two Puritans. The leader of the discussions is the apparently older and "wiser" Mr. Wiseman, who advises the spiritual stripling, Mr. Attentive. The latter is distressed about the "badness" of the times, and the reader can visualize the downward glance and the shaking of Wiseman's head as he responds that the times would mend if men would. In tones that are reminiscent of John Donne, he sighs for the man whose bell was tolled yesterday; and water stands in his eyes as he recalls that the deceased is damned. The two speakers sit under a tree, and Wiseman proceeds to distinguish which of the "Badmans" he means and to assert his own credentials as a narrator on the grounds that he was present at the death and had observed the life of the subject closely from its childhood. Ignoring Attentive's hope that he will speedily describe the death scene, Wiseman traces the "rake's progress"[1] of Badman from boyhood onward.

Badman was destined to be a leader but in an unfortunate direction: he was a ringleader in boyish mischief and became the "arch" among his adolescent friends. Wiseman enumerates Badman's sins (lying, stealing, hating and abusing the Sabbath, cursing and swearing, drinking, and whoring) and uses each as an occasion for sermonizing. Illustrative and often scintillating anecdotes abound under each topic, and Wiseman sometimes introduces meandering digressions. Attentive shows throughout a propensity to stand on moral absolutes and to jump to moral conclusions, and his supposition of parental blame for Badman's case must be checked by Wiseman's dissertation on the goodness of the parents of the title character. His father finally apprentices the boy to a good, devout, and merciful master, but to no avail. Badman runs away several times and eventually transfers to an evil master; again and again, he seems naturally drawn to evil. He outrascals this rascal (his master), and their relationship is tumultuous, but Badman completes his apprenticeship. The audience has little doubt by now that Badman was predestined to damnation and that he is the opposite of Christian of *The Pilgrim's Progress,* Part I.

Badman displays his histrionic bent when he returns home the reformed and model son, a role continued until his father lays out a sum to set him up in business. But Attentive is quick to condemn the parent for not testing his son's sincerity. Wiseman feels, alas, that Attentive has never known or has forgotten the "bowels" (a term prominent in *The Pilgrim's Progress,* Part II) or compassion of a father.

After about two and one-half years, with the help of his profligate friends, Badman is keeping his creditors at bay by the hint that he will make a rich marriage. At this point, he acts wonderfully the part of a repentant sinner to captivate a wealthy and pious young lady whose parents are dead. Having at length secured her, he abandons his religious guise; uses her money to pay off his creditors; returns to his old friends, haunts, and "drabs" (or whores); and frequently comes home drunk. He stops his wife's churchgoing and other pious activities; and, when she occasionally rebels, he threatens to inform the authorities of her conventicles. Nonetheless, the pair manages to produce seven children: one takes after the mother and is, accordingly, hated by Badman; three follow their father; and the others are in-between's or "mongrel professors." In the recital of these events, Wiseman has called attention to two especially heinous crimes of Badman: his hypocrisy in religion and his threat to betray his own wife and other Nonconformists for their unauthorized worship services. The fact that he merely *threatens,* however, may be Bunyan's way of allowing some merit to the most reprobate; and the reader is led to recall how fair Bunyan tried to be to the false pilgrims of *The Pilgrim's Progress,* Part I.

In condemning Badman, Bunyan now prepares to comment on the commercial interests of the Puritan community and to suggest, by contrast, a work ethic compatible with Puritan theology. Eventually, Badman is again in debt and must become a fawner on other men. There are rumors that he occasionally plays the highwayman.

His expedient this time is to go deeply in debt, declare bankruptcy, and get away with more money than he had, a ruse that is repeated on several occasions thereafter. In addition to beguiling his creditors, he cheats his customers by using deceitful weights and measures and by becoming adept at sleight of hand. He is a skillful extortioner: he takes advantage of customers' necessities by charging outlandish sums; he buys men's goods wholesale and then resells to them at unfair prices. Bunyan paints an impressively realistic picture of sharp practices of the day.

Before continuing the narrative of the marriage, Wiseman declaims on Badman's pride, malice, and envy; and he merges story and doctrine with his account of sickbed repentance. Twice the villain worries about his spiritual condition — once when he breaks his leg as he returns drunk from the tippling-house and again when he becomes sick, as he believes, to the death. He has his wife and her preachers and friends pray over him. When he recovers the last time and renews his old sins, the virtuous wife is so overcome that she dies, but only after admonitions to her family that effect the conversion of one child. Poetic justice finds Badman, however, though he is heard occasionally after her death to commend his good wife. This time a "quean" or whore tricks him into marriage and treats him as contemptibly as he has treated his first mate. After fourteen to sixteen years of mutual hate, these two part as "poor as howlets."

Wiseman at last arrives at the death scene, the part of the story for which Attentive has yearned. The dropsical, consumptive, surfeited, gouty, and (perhaps) pox-ridden Badman dies; when still a relatively young man; and he begins to stink and rot before he has been buried seventeen days.[2] The climactic revelation is that Badman, unlike his wicked brother, who died in despair, dies quietly, like a lamb or "chrisom-child." Thus his decease serves notice that a destination of heaven or hell cannot be adjudged by the behavior at death. The interlocutors, seeing that the sun grows low, part company; each, no doubt, is to continue to ruminate about this strange life and death of Mr. Badman.

II *The Form and Genre*

The novellike and nonallegorical *The Life and Death of Mr. Badman* is Bunyan's one major work in dialogue form, though *Instruction for the Ignorant* (a "catechism") in 1675 and *A Christian Dia-*

logue in 1666–1672 were earlier efforts of this type. Some of the conversations of Part I of *The Pilgrim's Progress* may also have contributed to the form of *Mr. Badman*. Its closest source is Arthur Dent's *The Plaine Mans Pathway to Heaven*,[3] which is a colloquy with four rather than two participants and which discusses many of the "sins" described in Bunyan's book.

According to the introduction, the success of Part I of *The Pilgrim's Progress* encouraged Bunyan to try to present the road to hell. It also entices the reader with the (unfulfilled) hope that Bunyan may one day write of those left behind Badman. Clearly, Bunyan intended the work to be exemplary in a negative way; like many of the minor characters of *The Pilgrim's Progress*, Badman shows the convertite how *not* to get to heaven. At the same time, his antics endow the book with the flavor of popular ballad and of the literature of the rogue.

The contemporary audience would also have been attracted by the hint of the introduction that *Badman* is another piece of the "literature of judgment," popular and often dramatic portrayals of an angry God dispensing justice to sinners. One of the best known of these "judgment" works is Samuel Clark's *Mirrour for Saints and Sinners,* which is frequently cited by Bunyan in *The Life and Death of Mr. Badman.*[4] This genre probably goes back to the exempla used in medieval sermons and to Renaissance mirror literature. Influence also came from natural human curiosity about sensational and prurient crimes, such as those revealed in John Reynolds' *The Triumphs of Gods Revenge Against ... Murther* (1621), which was made even more popular by the play *The Changeling* (1624) of Thomas Middleton and William Rowley. Bunyan himself displays a keen interest in Badman's violations of the sexual code, and his details of the ravages of the pox would scare any class of "hygiene" students today.

Critics rate rather highly the contributions of *Badman* to the development of the novel. Jack Lindsay considers it, in fact, the first realistic novel;[5] and Maurice Hussey finds it strange that Arthur Dent should exert so much influence on this "modern novel."[6] Many, contrastingly, are put off by the monotony of its morality and by its digressions; they wish, with Attentive, that Wiseman would "get on" to the death throes of Badman. And L. D. Lerner, one of its most negative critics, points out that the narrative basis "is so flimsy that the order of many episodes could be changed with no noticeable loss."[7] While there is truth in this criticism, Bunyan was hampered by the dialogue framework. Moreover, he may have feared, as some of his contemporaries had indicated, that he had already come too close to writing a "romance" in Part I of *The Pilgrim's Progress.*

III   *Commentary on the Times*

One of the most interesting features of this work is its many references to the badness of the times,[8] but the evil people are generalized because of Bunyan's position in the introduction that he will identify persons only if their names are already widely known. He does go so far as to set one crime in "Oliver's [Oliver Cromwell's] days," but the introduction gives a conventional picture of an England shaking and tottering with the burden (perhaps a recollection of Christian's in *The Pilgrim's Progress,* Part I) of Badman and his compeers. Singled out as especial sins of the day are cursing — man is the image of God, and to curse man is therefore to curse God; bad masters, who are interested only in worldly concerns and thus corrupt others as the sons of Eli corrupted their congregation; bad servants; "uncleanness"; the failure of children to heed their elders; spiritual inequality in marriage, which anticipates the plight of Mercy's sister Bountiful in *The Pilgrim's Progress,* Part II, and strikes a quite Miltonic note: "It is a deadly thing, I see, to be unequally yoked with unbelievers";[9] pride; and extortion. The last subject, extortion, forms one of the most important sections of the book and has attracted wide notice.

From "hucksters" and pawnbrokers of his day, Bunyan moves to a discussion of trading generally and has Wiseman provide instructions for righteous bartering. This practicality and application mark the work and are not unusual in light of such biblical minutia as crop rotation, rights of slaves, and rules governing usury and in light of the growth of commercialism among the middle-class Puritans, some of whom had come to believe that success in trade was a sign of their election. Bunyan has moved from spiritual autobiography in *Grace Abounding* and from the allegorizing and the universalizing of Part I of *The Pilgrim's Progress* to a work that centers on the lives of the Puritan businessmen and shopkeepers and that discourses on the intertwining of religion and work ethics.

Strangely, this topical section that is most in the tradition of the satire of manners has given rise to a feeling for Bunyan's modernity[10] and economic relevance. George Bernard Shaw calls *The Life and Death of Mr. Badman* a first-rate economic document;[11] he finds it up-to-date in 1914–1945, and feels that, during the nineteenth century, some of the largest London businesses were based on the kind of professional bankruptcy depicted by Bunyan.

IV   *The Style and the Bunyanesque Themes*

Badman is an entertaining work. Its prose is often rhythmic and felicitous, as in Wiseman's description of the title character ("Sin, sin, and to do the thing that was naught, was that which he delighted in, and that from a little child")[12] and in the introduction ("O debauchery, debauchery, what hast thou done in England!!"). The biblical echoes and proverbs are authentically Bunyanesque: "Sins go not alone, but follow one the other as do the links of a chain...."[13] Also present is the favored proverb of the dog who returns to its vomit as the type of the convert who falls to his old sins. The persistent Bunyan interests are here, too, such as the image of the spider's web[14] and the love of harmony in the story of the godly old Puritan at whose death sweet music was heard. There is the typical grumble at the Catholics in the section on swearing: "Some, indeed, swear by idols, as by the mass, by our lady, by saints, beasts, birds, and other creatures; but the usual way of our profane ones in England is to swear by God, Christ, faith, and the like."[15]

The citations of Scripture are so numerous that verisimilitude is amusingly shattered, since it is virtually impossible to imagine Wiseman remembering all of these references, chapter and verse. And, like Bunyan, Wiseman occasionally suffers slips of the memory in recalling them. Nonetheless, biblical verses are cleverly drawn into the story at some points, as, for example, when Bunyan presents a harsh reinterpretation of Hamor and Shechem's using religion and God as a "stalking horse," a favorite phrase of Bunyan, to get Jacob's daughters. The incident becomes a parallel for the way Badman traps his first wife and is thus more imaginatively applied than in the "theological" discussion of By-ends, Money-love, Save-all, and Hold-the-world in Part I of *The Pilgrim's Progress.*

V *Biographical Parallels*

There are some revealing biographical details in *Badman*. It is a
commonplace of criticism, for example, that at least a few of the
crimes of young Badman, particularly swearing, are those projected by the unregenerate Bunyan of the first pages of *Grace
Abounding*. And the response of "H. S." to the rebuke of his ways
— "What would the devil do for company if it was not for such as
I?"[16] — is a duplication of an anecdote in the spiritual
autobiography.

Bunyan drops the guise of Narrator Wiseman for a moment to
recount the story of the "troubled woman" who visited him in
prison and who feared that she would be damned for robbing the
shopkeeper with whom she had formerly lived. The reader is
pleased to discover here proof of Bunyan's fame as a counselor and
as a soul-healer; and he is amused by the revelation that, as sus-
pected, "Wiseman" is a persona for the author.[17] As in *Grace
Abounding,* however, there is nothing self-serving about such mild
braggadocio; for Wiseman indulges in the now familiar down-
grading of his education and abilities: ". . . as for the proud dames
in England that profess, they have Moses and the prophets, and if
they will not hear them, how then can we hope that they should
receive good by such a dull-sounding ram's horn as I am?"[18] It
should be pointed out, even so, that "ram's horn" puts him in the
company of God's Old Testament vehicles of truth. In *A Few Sighs
from Hell* (1658), moreover, Bunyan strikes the typical Puritan
note of pride in the humble voice and plain style; and, as he does in
The Pilgrim's Progress, Part I, he lashes out at gentlemen: "Take
notice of this, you that are despisers of the least of the Lazaruses of
our Lord Jesus Christ; it may be now you are loth to receive these
little ones of his, because they are not gentlemen, because they
cannot, with Pontius Pilate, speak Hebrew, Greek, and Latin."[19]

Bunyan must also be recalling his own early reading interests in
Badman's "beastly romances, and books full of ribaldry." Though
Arthur Dent's *The Plaine Mans Pathway to Heaven* contains a
similar passage, an admission in *A Few Sighs from Hell* confirms
Bunyan's originality: ". . . the Scriptures, thought I, what are they?
A dead letter, a little ink and paper, of three or four shillings price.
Alas! What is the Scripture? Give me a ballad, a news-book,
George on horseback, or Bevis of Southampton; give me some
book that teaches curious arts, that tells of old fables; but for the

holy Scriptures I cared not."[20]

One of the great curiosities of *Badman* has always been the quiet demise of the protagonist, who, by rights, should suffer some fore-taste of the agonies of hellfire. The Renaissance had relied on deathbed actions as the key to a man's life: he who had lived well died well. In *Grace Abounding,* Bunyan seems to acknowledge this dictum in admitting his fear in prison that he could not act man-fully during torture and death. By the writing of *Badman,* he had recanted this view; and he censors Attentive's keenness to know how Badman died and the contemporary tendency to preempt God's judgment by evaluating the dying on the basis of "proper" deathbed behavior. Bunyan may well have felt that some of the brethren had gone so far as to use deathbed actions as indications of election or reprobation and that both writers and readers needed to be reminded that God's ways are inscrutable. At least, a major point of *Badman* is the futility of judging a man's life by his con-duct in dying. And, artistically, the ending serves to offset the fre-quent charge that Bunyan drew only types. The fact that the bad man does not die badly is realistic.

VI *Psychological Insight*

There is a certain amount of psychological insight into the character of Badman, whose cursing and swearing, carefully distin-guished "arts" as Wiseman presents them, are a badge of manly honor, perhaps another recollection of Bunyan's own motivations as a youth. Badman's actions when forced to attend church are droll and thoroughly believable; and Bunyan probably had wit-nessed similar antics among the members of his own congregations — Badman sleeps, lusts after "beautiful objects," whispers, gig-gles, or plays. Moreover, though Bunyan is at a disadvantage in having to present his title character through the descriptions of Wiseman, Badman is a credible and real figure, despite the impedi-ment of his name. Bunyan seems to have found this indirection no great setback, for he manages a similar task in *The Holy War,* where Emmanuel is kept offstage so much of the time and yet is so functional throughout. Nonetheless, the reader misses the intimacy and concern that he shared with Christian, who did not know whether he had been predestined to election or damnation. Still, Christian often seems simplistic beside Badman.

The participants in the dialogue are not entirely cardboard figures. Wiseman is endowed with a certain air of priggishness as if to suggest that Bunyan was not unaware that the moral earnestness of the Puritans must sometimes appear hypocritical to others. Attentive, too, is cleverly drawn, though he smacks of the ingenuous straight man of traditional literary dialogues. Humor is present and there is perhaps a sly self-mocking in Bunyan's having Attentive try to hurry Wiseman on to the "interesting part." At the same time, the ruse is skillful and drives toward the climax: Badman's deportment at his physical death is of little consequence, for he has always been spiritually dead.

VII   *The Anecdotes*

Bunyan indulged himself in *The Life and Death of Mr. Badman* in quite a number of ancillary biographies or exemplary anecdotes within the large biography of the principal knave. Lying is decried through the tale of Ananias and Sapphira. The story of Old Tod, adapted by Robert Browning in his poem "Ned Bratts," demonstrates the "rewards" of stealing. Like Badman, Old Tod began his sinful career as a child. Finally, driven by despair of his spiritual condition and dressed in his green suit, perhaps an echo of the Robin Hood legends, he appeared at the summer assizes with his wife to announce their guilt; and both were hanged. Tod is the embodiment of Bunyan's ever-present fear that repentance might come "too late."

The fate of those who curse and swear is put forth in three main sketches: the death of "N. P." after a bout of cursing and swearing; the well-developed narration of Dorothy Mately's sinking into the ground;[21] and the abuse of his foolish son Ned by the keeper of the "blind ale-house," who could not be exorcized of the Devil and died horribly. As a coda for these "local" illustrations, Bunyan uses the example of Judas to affirm the continuity between the Bible and everyday life. Several "devil-snatchings" also demonstrate the folly of swearing.

The perils of drunkenness are set forth in the account of the master who sends his drunken groom to learn wisdom from the horse, which drinks only to satisfy thirst. Later in *Badman,* Bunyan couples drinking with doubt of the reality of God or the Devil in three anecdotes that he says he borrowed from Samuel Clark's *Mirrour for Saints and Sinners.* The trick is to get the culprit vaingloriously to swear that the Devil does not exist or to dare Old Nick to drink with him, and the results are akin to the scheme manipulated by Satan in Chaucer's *The Friar's Tale.*

Of the some eight anecdotes demonstrating the dangers of whoring, two are outstanding, the first for its macabre humor. A man almost loses his sight from the pox; and, when his physicians tell him that he must give up women, he responds: "Nay then . . . farewell sweet sight."[22] The tale is reminiscent of the accusation that Milton's blindness resulted from his "haunting the bordellos" and of the taunt in Sir John Suckling's "A Session of the Poets" that William D'Avenant lost his nose through syphilis and the mercury treatments he took to cure it. Bunyan probably had no knowledge of Suckling or of Milton (though some believe that *Paradise Lost* was a great influence on *The Holy War*), but he is remarkable in *Badman* for turning the literature of "prurience" into propaganda for reformation.

The second outstanding illustration of whoring is grotesque. An acquaintance of Wiseman has a mother who is a midwife and who was spirited off by a young gallant to deliver his illegitimate child, which he immediately threw into the fire to cover his foulness. The accompanying biblical example this time is positive, for Wiseman recalls one of Bunyan's favorite stories, how Joseph withstood Potiphar's wife.

An incidental and highly fetching "homily," no doubt as much for Attentive as for the audience in general, is used to show that good parents cannot always control their children. A devout mother prays and prays for her evil son but to no avail. In despair of his reformation, she finally tells him that she will rejoice when he is damned; and the miscreant is thereupon converted.

The informers who plagued Bunyan and his followers and all holders of conventicles are pinpointed in the story of "W. S.,"[23] whose betrayal of others causes him to be stricken with a faltering tongue and whose condition worsens until he cannot speak at all and finally dies. Another such talebearer is presented by Bunyan as being bitten by his own dog and as dying of gangrene. Such examples of God's poetic justice are not the product of the "mechanick" minds alone, for one has only to recall the jewel struck to commemorate the English victory over the Spanish Armada. On one side is the expected portrait of Queen Elizabeth; on the other, the Ark being blown to safety by a wind from heaven. The whole period was aware of the force of God in the affairs of the world.

The last two stories, of the barber who cut his throat and of John

Cox's disembowelment, are so ensanguined, particularly the latter with its self-laceration and the blood covering the walls of the room, as to convince the reader that Attentive knows what to expect when he keeps wanting to get on to the death part. Embedded between Wiseman's two descriptions of the quiet death of Badman, these scenes of carnage have an overwhelming impact and attest to Bunyan's growing grasp of the dramatic — here in the use of the principle of contrast. Of the major works of Bunyan, *The Life and Death of Mr. Badman* is the one that was most intended to have wide popular appeal. Bunyan must have felt that, while his audience would be lured first by the violence and lickerishness, it would also absorb the messages of the book.

CHAPTER 5

The Holy War

I   *The Narration*

BUNYAN returns to allegory and to a first-person narration in *The Holy War* (1682). His opening suggests, however, that he will treat not only the universal theme of the title but also individual conversion and life in a Nonconformist area like Bedfordshire. In his travels, the narrator comes to the continent of Universe and the town or "corporation" of Mansoul, where Shaddai or God has a palace, the heart. This town, the body, is walled; and its five entrances, the senses — Ear-, Eye-, Mouth-, Nose-, and Feel-gate — cannot be penetrated without the townsmen's consent. Already, Bunyan reminds his Puritan audience of the need for alertness and right thinking.

In recording the background of Mansoul, Bunyan unfolds an account of the War in Heaven and of its consequences very similar to that of Milton in *Paradise Lost*. The giant Diabolus, Bunyan's Satan figure, was present when Mansoul was built; he has since assaulted King Shaddai's Son, whom Bunyan calls "Emmanuel," and has been punished for his treason by being enchained and banished to the pits. Diabolus calls his coconspirators to a council of war to decide upon methods of revenge. Mansoul has been built for Shaddai's own delight, and the devils decide that taking it will be the sweetest kind of revenge. Diabolus, as a dragon, and the other devils, who are invisible, draw up before Ear-gate; logically, if the ear can activate faith (as the Puritans believed), it can also be used to pervert it.

Using Ill-pause as his orator, Diabolus parleys with the chiefs of the town, who come to the wall. While Ill-pause and Diabolus wheedle the Mansoulians into believing that Shaddai would keep them ignorant, an argument similar to one Milton's Satan uses on Eve, the Fury Tisiphone kills Resistance. The people then eat of the leaves of a tree and Innocency dies; for Bunyan ignores Adam and Eve to place more emphasis on the community of mankind, who become drunken as a consequence of their feast and willfully open Ear- and Eye-gate to receive Diabolus. Striking quickly, Diabolus deposes Mayor Understanding and Recorder Conscience and, by his rhetoric, wins over Lord Will-be-will, Clerk Mind, and Deputy Vile-Affection. The image of Shaddai is defaced by No-truth, and one of Diabolus is set up. Lord Lustings, who is eyeless and earless, becomes mayor; Forget-good, the recorder; and thirteen new aldermen are appointed, among whom are Whoring and Incredulity. Strongholds are set up; and Mansoul becomes the "den" and "hold" of Diabolus, in images recalling the opening of Part I of *The Pilgrim's Progress*. Worth noting, too, is the use of provincial governmental terms that assure an understanding on the part of the simplest people of Bedford.

Meanwhile, a heavenly messenger carries the story of Mansoul's conquest to Shaddai; but the King and His Son have foreknowledge of the situation and, like Milton's Father and Son, have reached an agreement about the consequences for man. Diabolus represses this news, intensifies his fortification of Ear-gate and Eye-gate, and makes the Mansoulians sign a covenant, a parody of God's covenant with the Chosen People and of the covenant of redemption sealed by Christ's sacrifice. He enlists the aid of Mr. Filth, and such license is allowed the inhabitants of the town that Diabolus is in fair hopes of Shaddai's forsaking them. Diabolus addresses them in the marketplace on the terrors of their former Lord and decks them out in his own armor, a caricature of Paul's "whole armor of God."

Shaddai, however, does not relinquish Mansoul. Symbolically, he first tries to recall it through the "terrors of the Law." He sends an army of over forty thousand, led by four captains — Boanerges, Conviction, Judgment, and Execution — each of whom has an ensign, colors, and an escutcheon. They arrive at Ear-gate and try for three days to parley with Mansoul, sending out first the trumpeter Take-heed-what-you-hear. Each of the captains in turn addresses the city; but finally, directed by Diabolus, the Mansoulians give Shaddai's troops three days to depart. The city's defenses, especially Ear-gate, are readied, and the "holy war" begins.

In their winter quarters, the attackers are joined by Tradition, Human Wisdom, and Man's Invention; but Diabolus captures this threesome and persuades its members to join him. Within the city, however, there are changes of heart and jarrings by Conscience. Famine weakens the Mansoulians; and Boanerges keeps urging them to surrender, each time sending a harsher messenger. Mansoul parleys but sets ridiculous conditions and is rebuked by Boanerges. Fighting breaks out among the inhabitants of Mansoul, and the mischief of Incredulity in arousing the town against Shaddai is momentarily stopped.

Mansoul seems torn between Diabolus, who imprisons Understanding and Conscience and persuades the Mansoulians to "harden their hearts," and Boanerges, who sends more entreaties to Ear-gate and prays to Shaddai for help through a petition carried by Love-to-man. The Son is ready and exhilarated as he sets out in response. He is accompanied by Captains Credence, Goodhope, Charity, Innocence, and Patience and by numerous *reformades,* or volunteers; and he has forty-four golden battering rams and twelve golden slings. Emmanuel, like Boanerges, approaches the townsmen progressively, using a white flag and three doves to show his good intentions, then a red, and finally a black flag. The reader begins to suspect that Bunyan has read or heard about Christopher Marlowe's *Tamburlaine,* Part I, and its use of similar colors before the walls of Damascus.

Diabolus talks with Emanuel but in the "language of the infernal pit," so that the Mansoulians are ignorant of the Son's rebuke of the Devil and of his assertion of Shaddai's claim to the town. Words cease and the battle begins — a sight to see, the narrator indicates, with "wounds aplenty" on both sides. After the fight, Emmanuel again runs out the white flag as a token of his kindliness toward the inmates of Mansoul. Diabolus tries a promise of reformation to get the siege lifted, but the Prince is too wise for him and is unlike the many taken in by the histrionics of Badman in Bunyan's earlier work. Battle resumes and Diabolus, seeing how it will end, cautions his troops to do as much harm to Mansoul as possible before they are driven out. Ear-gate is taken, and the Recorder's house becomes Emmanuel's quarters. Strict orders are issued by the Prince to hurt the Diabolonians but to spare the Mansoulians.

When the city is taken, its chief men petition Emmanuel for mercy; but, in his triumphant march through the streets, the people are unable to read his countenance. Diabolus is stripped of his armor and bound to Emmanuel's chariot. The victor then retires to his quarters outside the city and greets petitioners, apparently impassively. Eventually, however, he makes an appointment with the suppliants for the next day. When they arrive, anticipating death, they are forgiven and receive a parchment sealed with seven seals, an image from Daniel and Revelation that Bunyan had also adopted in *Grace Abounding* and *The Pilgrim's Progress,* Part I. In terms of Christian history, the Redemption has arrived. The suppliants are piped and tabored back to Mansoul and to the waiting people, who receive the news of their deliverance with bells, music, and joy. The Mansoulians invite Emmanuel to live with them and are feasted by him with *outlandish* ("heavenly") food.

Reformation of Mansoul is the next order of business. Understanding again becomes mayor; and Conscience, who is displaced from his original task as Recorder by Knowledge, is promised another position. Diabolus' image and his three strongholds are destroyed. With a reversal of the situation in *The Pilgrim's Progress,* Part I, good tries evil in a jury trial of such leading Diabolonians and false Mansoulians as have been caught; and most of the prisoners are crucified. Incredulity escapes to Diabolus. Experience is made a captain, and a new charter for the city (the New Testament? the founding of the Church and the community of believers?) is drawn up and engraved on the gates. The Mansoulians are given two teachers, Holy Spirit and Conscience, and are warned that they will be assailed by such henchmen of Diabolus as Witchcraft, Heresy, and Revelling. In more images from Revelation, Emmanuel dresses his townsmen in white; and they are feasted every day and given sacramental gifts. This peace lasts all summer; and then the town heeds Carnal-security, whose father was a Diabolonian. Emmanuel returns to his Father in something of a huff, and Godly-fear tries to bring the people to their senses. Sickness breaks out, and many unheeded petitioners are sent to heaven. During the ensuing sharp, cold, and tedious winter, the Diabolonians, whom the Mansoulians have failed to root out, begin to work on the people.

Profane, representing the Diabolonians within Mansoul, delivers a request for advice to the False Prince and strikes up a pleasing acquaintance with Cerberus, the porter of hell. In an infernal council, Diabolus decides to have Lasciviousness, Covetousness, and Anger disguise themselves as servants and infiltrate Mansoul. Fortunately, Pry-well overhears the machinations of the Diabolonians at Vile-hill and is rewarded for his report to the City Fathers with the office of Scout-master-general to search out the enemy.

Diabolus appoints Incredulity as his general; and nine captains (including Rage, who commands the Election-doubters; Fury; Damnation; Insatiable; and Brimstone) are named. Beelzebub, Lucifer, Legion, Apollyon, Python, Cerberus, and Belial are to rule the captains. Diabolus tries parleying with the city and sets up special forces at the gates, but Mansoul manages to get messages to Emmanuel through Mouth-gate. Again, there are many wounded on both sides. The Mansoulians foolishly send out an attack party against Diabolus by night, and it is routed.

Then the False Prince and his army of Doubters (of the Redemption) break through Feel-gate and ravish the women, but a number of the Mansoulians hold out in the castle for about two and one-half years; Bunyan perhaps remembered an especially trying period of despair recorded in *Grace Abounding*. Credence delivers a request to Shaddai, and Emmanuel sends back a packet of letters. Increased persecution for this overture to heaven having failed, Diabolus calls another council; and, when get-rich-quick schemes are selected as the next tactic, Bunyan alludes again to the commercial gains made by Puritan society. Meanwhile, a letter announces that Emmanuel will join the Mansoulians on the third day as Bunyan indulges in some of his more obvious number symbolism, and the town rejoices. The ensuing battle ends victoriously for Emmanuel, the Doubters are destroyed, and the Prince again enters the town in triumph. A burial detail is charged to find every piece of Doubter and destroy it.

Diabolus and Incredulity retreat to Hell-gate Hill and then to the Devil's den to plot. This time they send out Doubters and Blood-men. The fight is on: the Doubters straggle off; and the Bloodmen are taken alive, in accordance with the orders of Emmanuel, and are bound over to answer at the assizes (the Last Judgment). These Bloodmen may represent those who persecute the faithful and, specifically, those in Charles II's England who persecuted Nonconformists. Security is again short-lived, however, as Diligence overhears Evil-questioning plotting with the Doubters. Another trial is held, and the convicted ones are put to death. Other Diabolonians are sought out, but Carnal-sense escapes to lurk in dens in Mansoul. The narrator appears to have been forgotten as a long, elegant, and apocalyptic speech by Emmanuel finishes the story; and the inhabitants of Mansoul learn that he lets Diabolus live to keep man watchful, another Miltonic note.

II *The Allegory*

Thomas Babington Macaulay's view that "...the *Holy War* ... if the *Pilgrim's Progress* did not exist, would be the best allegory that ever was written"[1] is shared by George Offor, who calls this work Bunyan's "most profound and beautiful allegory" and "one of the most perfect of allegories."[2] And G. B. Harrison, though he feels that the reader is apt to spend too much time on its "astonishing ingenuity," acquiesces; he finds it, as a work of art, "the greatest English allegory."[3] Others who are less impressed have explored its confusion of allegorical levels[4] or its simplicity of allegorical approach.[5] George Bernard Shaw found its theology repellent and the book "hardly readable."[6]

As with the pilgrimage of life in *The Pilgrim's Progress,* Bunyan chose for *The Holy War* a universal metaphor. In keeping with the military imagery of the Pauline Epistles, devotional writers have often likened the soul to a town under siege. The Puritans in particular thought of themselves as soldiers of Christ, and Cromwell's special troops could preach *and* fight. As a result, it is probably unfruitful to belabor the derivativeness of *The Holy War,* although *Paradise Lost*[7] and Richard Bernard's *The Isle of Man*[8] are considered to have been influences. Among other works often cited for comparison are Thomas Fuller's *A History of the Holy War,* Phineas Fletcher's *Purple Island,* and Prudentius' *Psychomachia.* It should not be forgotten, however, that Bunyan's own earlier work, *The Holy City; Or, The New Jerusalem* (1665), as well as the influence of Revelation on *The Pilgrim's Progress,* reveals Bunyan's imaginative interest in similar ideas and materials.

The allegory of *The Holy War* is vast, sprawling, and multileveled; but this complexity would not have been strange to Bunyan's reading public; the Puritans, though they placed most emphasis on a literal meaning, could also draw upon other levels of the medieval four-fold interpretation of Scripture. Bunyan does so, for example, in using Revelation and the Song of Songs in *The Pilgrim's Progress* and in his works on Solomon's temple. In *The Holy War,* though Bunyan maintains a corporate identity — the individual soul has become Mansoul or all men — his own religious experience and the typical Puritan pattern of conversion are also present. *The Holy War* has, then, an intricate link with *Grace Abounding* and *The Pilgrim's Progress.*[9]

On another level, Bunyan traces the history of the Church, which becomes the spouse of Christ, just as it does in *The Pilgrim's Progress,* Part I. Still another focus resides in biblical experience, for the consistently Christ-possessed Bunyan moves in this work from the Old Testament rigors of the Law to the Gospel dispensation of Christ and to the "general pardon" that Christ offers to all but the Diabolonians. Finally, *The Holy War* is a product of its milieu, for it has a strong millenarian theme, since Christ dwells for a time in Mansoul, leaves it to renewed persecution, and drives the Devil off once again. The story must, of course, end realistically with Emmanuel's promise to come again rather than with the actual establishment of the New Jerusalem. The Fifth Monarchists may have claimed that the Commonwealth would be succeeded by the reign of Jesus on earth, but Bunyan was too practical to draw conclusions about God's own time.

Many of the confusions in *The Holy War* derive from this millenarianism. For example, it is strange to find a feast of hospitality (a standard symbol for the Lord's Supper and the Marriage Supper of the Lamb) remain literal. In contrast, in Part I of *The Pilgrim's Progress,* Christian's sharing of meals and his "marriage with the Lamb" at death symbolize the ultimate union of Christ with his Church and redemption through the Judgment. In *The Holy War,* Emmanuel treats Mansoul to *heavenly* food (the water made into wine, the "angels' cates" or manna from Heaven, and the "honey from the rock"). The reader expects, therefore, that the reign of Christ on earth has begun; but the end precludes such a precise interpretation. The only reasonable alternative is that Bunyan is presenting the indwelling of Christ in the heart of man.

A similar difficulty arises when one of Emmanuel's gifts to the Mansoulians, a ring, presumably symbolizes marriage of the soul with Christ at the death of the elect. The point is that, while the reader can grapple with the allegory of *The Pilgrim's Progress,* where the protagonists die and make their individual leaps into Christ's bosom, he falters if he marches too steadily on the allegorical trail of *The Holy War.* Only Conscience approaches death and strikes similarities with Christian: "And, Mr. Recorder, because thou art old, and through many abuses made feeble, therefore I give thee leave and license to go when thou wilt to my fountain, my conduit, and there to drink freely of the blood of my grape...."[10] It is easy enough, perhaps, to pass off the dressing in white of the Mansoulians as the rite of sanctification, as in *The Pilgrim's Prog-*

ress, Part II; but one cannot forget that this act is taken from Revelation where it is the reward of the redeemed at the Day of Judgment. For that matter, one does not forget that the parchment bound with seven seals and delivered as a pardon to the Mansoulians is also a pronouncement of woe and despair to the unredeemed of the Apocalypse.

Added to the perverseness of *The Holy War's* being and not being the story of the millennium and the Final Judgment, there are, again as in *The Pilgrim's Progress,* tendencies toward allegory within allegory: the Son's "leaping on the mountains" with joy, as prophesied in the Old Testament; the number symbolism of *three* to point up Christ's rising from the dead after three days; and the allegorical and emblematic flavor of the descriptions of Shaddai's, Emmanuel's, and Diabolus' captains. Then there is the strange fact that Diabolus' first act is to destroy the *image of* Shaddai. The reader can only presume that this last refers to the image of Christ in the heart, but there is no localization of the text within Heart Castle. Besides, if the allegory holds true, Bunyan is yet at the stage of the narrative under the dispensation of the Law.

Another curious instance of internal allegory occurs in the opening when the narrator indicates that he has learned the language of Mansoul and would have stayed there had the Master not called him home: "...yea, I had, to be sure, even lived and died a native among them (I was so taken with them and their doings,) had not my Master sent for me home to his house, there to do business for him, and to oversee business done." Bunyan is probably referring to his conversion and call to the ministry, but also present is the implication of leaving the follies of this world for the truth of the next (through death). *The Holy War,* then, is, in terms of its religious allegory, so incredibly complex that it needs intense study.

Difficulties of allegorical interpretation abound at the level of word choice itself. Though no one could hope for a more natural and soothing explanation for Diabolus' choosing the form of a dragon — "...for that it was in those days as familiar with the town of Mansoul as now is the bird with the boy"[11] — it simply calls up too many questions. Is the narrator talking of the time of fairy tales when dragons frequented the earth? Is his account set in a period before *dragon* became an epithet for the Devil? Is this episode an explanation of how the dragon became associated with Satan, as in Revelation? Is this an account of an event that happened in a time when man was so evil that he was naturally beset by

dragons? Presumably, the Mansoulians are still innocent when
Diabolus sets out to prevail upon them; and, while the reader can
take pleasure in the psychological subtlety of Diabolus' disguise, he
is forced to ponder its allegorical ramifications.

A safer course of interpretation of *The Holy War* for some
readers has been that of contemporary political allegory. George
Offor prefers this approach for all of Bunyan's works, but particularly for *The Holy War*. William York Tindall goes so far as to
identify the first reign of Diabolus with that of Charles I; the first
appearance of Emmanuel with the "rule of saints," (1649–1653; the
decline of the town with the decline of Cromwell; the return of
Diabolus with the Restoration; and the remodeling of Mansoul by
Diabolus with Charles II's purging of Nonconformists from the
English towns by reincorporating and imposing new charters.[12] The
Bloodmen may represent this last particular form of persecution,
and the deposing of the Recorder of Mansoul perhaps alludes to the
firing of Robert Audley from a similar position in Bedford. Roger
Sharrock further suggests that Filth is a satirization of Roger
L'Estrange, the licenser of the press who was especially severe with
Nonconformist works.[13] Certainly some of the war details are from
Bunyan's own experiences or from accounts he had heard, and the
Puritan New Model Army may have been in his mind when he
painted Shaddai's warriors. The trials, which are as vivid as that of
Faithful in Part I of *The Pilgrim's Progress,* surely recall Bunyan's
past entanglements with the law.

Time and again Bunyan demonstrates that he is not politically
controversial and insists that he is loyal to his kind. Perhaps, then,
Jack Lindsay overstates somewhat: "The bedrock of *The Holy
War* is ... an imaginative rendering of the conflict between the
King and the town of Bedford, absolutism against the liberties of
the people."[14] Bunyan does probably glance satirically and rebuk-
ingly at the conduct of the Royalists under the command of Prince
Rupert when he makes the point that Shaddai's men do not harm
the areas through which they march but live on "the King's cost";
and his several references to the "reformades" are doubtless also
drawn from direct experience. But there is no mention of "Oliver's
days" here, and Bunyan is generally content to paint life and religion in a contemporary English town. One senses that, mainly,
Bunyan had moved into his own element, as his language exudes
enthusiasm for the "battle parts," which are much more realistic
than Milton's in *Paradise Lost.* He addresses himself to the wars as

"a sight worth seeing" and invites, "Come up then to the mountains you that love to see military actions, and behold by both sides how the fatal blow is given...."[15]

III   *Style, General Atmosphere, and Characterization*

Some critics have considered *The Holy War* an epic, possibly as a result of its similarities in content to *Paradise Lost*. E. M. W. Tillyard insists that "No other work has so good a claim to be called England's Puritan epic."[16] Rather, it attempts to be "epic-like," as if Bunyan's increasing fame caused him unconsciously to strive for an ornate and "literary" style. He is more learned and classical than in previous works. In the Address to the Reader, he uses *primum mobile* for "soul" and mentions the topos of the "plurality of worlds." While both tags were popular throughout the Renaissance, they seem somewhat forced in the "plain style" of the Puritan. Moreover, Bunyan deliberately chooses less familiar and more formal titles for his chief figures, including the Hebraic "Shaddai" for God. Drawing on classical mythology, he places the Furies among his devils and makes Cerberus the porter of hell. He also evinces a fondness for lists, as if he knew of the epic convention of catalogs; and he uses "Item" as well.

Overall, however, there is a diminution of Bunyan's interest in or of his abilities to maintain the grand scheme of the struggle between the forces of Good and Evil for the soul of man. He tends to settle back into his popular and familiar idiom as often as possible and to emphasize, as in *Grace Abounding* and in *The Pilgrim's Progress,* the individual conversion experience. In fact, Bunyan apparently felt the strain of this complex work he was undertaking. There is an air of wistfulness at times when he admits that he would like to pursue some of his subordinate characters but realizes that he must plunge on with the main story ("But to pass by this"). Occasionally, the effort to keep all of the allegorical levels together becomes too much: "He told too, the which I had almost forgot, how Diabolus had put the town of Mansoul into arms...."[17] The literary craftsmanship that began to develop in the writing of *Grace Abounding,* however, checks this laxity by such leisurely introductions as "Well, upon a time...."

Characterization, except in the cases of Diabolus and Emmanuel, is usually confined to bringing to life "ticket-names," but a minor character can leap forth by a judicious choice of words or by his

posturing. Lord Love-flesh is a "fellow [who] could find more
sweetness when he stood sucking of a lust, than he did in all the
paradise of God."[18] Wet-eyes, one of Mansoul's ambassadors to
Emmanuel, comes into the Presence wringing his heads and saying
that his mother named him, but he does not know whether for the
moistness of his brain or the softness of his heart. Will-be-will, the
advocate of free will, uses "big and ruffling words." Lucifer is not
only an orator but a prodigious correspondent who begins his
epistle to Anything with "Anything [a pun?], my darling"; and he
closes one to the Mansoulians with "All the blessings of the pit be
upon you...." Diabolus' henchmen are fond of making their
leader a "low congé" or bow, and they activate themselves only
after "a Diabolonian ceremony or two." Bunyan apparently took
great pleasure in making his devils (and occasionally his angels) talk
and act like Restoration dandies even as he continued the attack on
glibness and finicalness that he had waged in Part I of *The Pilgrim's Progress.*

Diabolus, on the other hand, is a well-developed character of
great deviousness. He is a skillful rhetorician who often provides
himself with a backup man (for example, Ill-pause); and he is at his
best in the first attempt on Mansoul when he tells the townsmen in
effect that Shaddai would keep them in ignorance and slavery
through corrupt laws. He perverts before their very eyes as he
persuades the Mansoulians that the former Recorder, Conscience,
is an old and a crazy man whose frenzies should not be heeded. He
verbally attacks the Mansoulians with the epithet "runagates"; and
he also indulges in one of Bunyan's "scraps of Latin," *probatum
est,* used again in *The Water of Life* (1688),[19] to lend dignity and a
semblance of order to one of his infernal councils. The emotional
pitch of Diabolus' rhetoric in arousing the Diabolonians
demonstrates his scheming personality; and he frightens the
Mansoulians into believing that Shaddai will destroy them "root
and branch," a phrase that resonates with Puritan associations. He
also proclaims: "... blood, blood, nothing but blood is in every
blast of Shaddai's trumpet against poor Mansoul now."[20]

Bunyan's masterpiece is Emmanuel, a more beautiful if less
subtle and intellectual portrayal of God's Son than that in *Paradise
Lost.* As if Bunyan were in awe of his own presentation, he keeps
Emmanuel at a distance, and his golden entries are increasingly effective for their having been long anticipated. The most remarkable
instance of his character is the cat-and-mouse game he plays with

the Mansoulians when he captures the town. He is deliberately detached and cool to the townsmen, and Bunyan cites as a parallel Joseph's reception of his brothers in Egypt. Dramatically, however, he turns aside to weep over the petition of Desires-awake. Other memorable acts are his "leaping for joy on the mountains" and his remembering old Conscience.

Moreover, an untoppable rightness exists in the ending of Emmanuel's conversation with Diabolus: " 'And now,' said the golden-headed Prince, 'I have a word to the town of Mansoul....' "[21] It is almost as if Bunyan were familiar with George Chapman's view that Christ was the first gentleman, for the Son's "striking hands with the Father" puts their guarantee to save Mansoul into the nature of a gentlemen's agreement. But Emmanuel's language can become tough and almost colloquial at times, and one senses that Bunyan discontinues the "gentleman-ese" purposely in order to emphasize the perceptiveness of the young prince: "But if righteousness be such a beauty-spot in thine eyes now, how is it that wickedness was so closely stuck to by thee before."[22]

The narrator's language is generally distinctively different from that of individual speakers, and it has its own moods. Conjecturing about the death of Innocency, Bunyan chooses words that show his contempt for evil: "...whether by a shot from the camp of the giant, or from some sinking qualm ... or whether by the stinking breath of that treacherous villain old Illpause, for so I am most apt to think...."[23] In "an income that might have contented his Luciferian heart, had it not been insatiable...,"[24] he draws on the commercial rhetoric popular among the Puritans and on a happy conversion of proper noun to adjective to castigate Diabolus' rebellion against heaven and to recall the association of Apollyon with money in *The Pilgrim's Progress,* Part I. The rather loose adaptation of Scripture has a blunt power of its own when Diabolus is described as making Mansoul "like to a sensual sow," and the moral is sharply delineated in these summaries of Mansoul's decampment: "...the whole town of Mansoul was in her career after vanity, and in her dance after the giant's pipe" and "Nor did the silly Mansoul stick or boggle at all at this most monstrous engagement, but, as if it had been a sprat in the mouth of a whale, they swallowed it without any chewing."[25] As these passages indicate, the remoteness of allegory cannot throttle the authentic human voice in *The Holy War.*

IV   *Recurrent Bunyan Themes and Techniques*

In spite of its epiclike trappings and its grand scheme, *The Holy War* contains many evidences of the standard Bunyan. The author refers to the influence of books in the section dealing with Filth's proclamation allowing "odious and atheistical pamphlets, and filthy ballads and romances full of ribaldry,"[26] another recollection of Bunyan's and Badman's first "intellectual" nourishment. There is also the familiar scant but heated deprecation of the Catholics in Cerberus' oath, "By Saint Mary," and in the startling inclusion of "Pope," with his escutcheon of a stake, a flame, and "a good man in it," among the captains of the Bloodmen, all the rest of whom are biblical reprobates. The technique is quite as effective as Alexander Pope's use of zeugma in "The Rape of the Lock."

Proverbs and musical references are also supplied. One finds "striking while the iron is hot" and "taking pepper in the nose," as well as the proverbial tale of the Devil and the collier. Though the proverbs are less frequent in *The Holy War* than in previous works, Bunyan ingeniously converts them to names when Diabolus ensnares "Mr. Penny-wise-pound-foolish" and "Mr. Get-i'th-hundred-and-lose-i'th-shire" with his visions of fast money. Music always accompanies Emmanuel in triumph and Mansoul in happiness, and musicians from the court of Shaddai entertain the Mansoulians at the Prince's feast. Quite pleasing and humorous is Cerberus' assurance that hell will welcome Profane with "as good a coranto as this kingdom will afford."

If proverbs are in relatively short supply in *The Holy War,* riddles are more expansively used than before. They form part of the entertainment at Emmanuel's feast where they represent Scripture and recall Bunyan's remarks about riddles and his allegorical method in the preface to *The Pilgrim's Progress,* Part I. And in the Doubters' straggling off by *fives, nines,* and *seventeens,* there seems to be a "numerical" riddle that is the result of Bunyan's adopting the fashion of the "number of the beast" in Daniel and Revelation.

Bunyan suggests that the whole work is a riddle for which his "window" is the key:

> Nor do thou go to work without my key,
> (In mysteries men do often lose their way,)
> And also turn it right; if thou wouldst know
> My riddle, and with my heifer plow,
> It lies there in the window.

Critics have assumed that he means by "window" his marginal notations, but he may have introduced a quibble here because "window" also refers to both the Address and the Advertisement to the Reader. In other words, the method for unraveling the work is demonstrated by the process of riddle-solving put forth in these two ancillary poems.

In the Advertisement, after asserting that both *The Pilgrim's Progress,* Part I, and *The Holy War* are his own works, he concludes with his name in anagram: "Witness my name, if ana-grammed to thee, / The letters make, Nu hony in a B." This "new honey in a bee" refers to Samson's riddle of the bees and the honey in the carcass of the lion, and Bunyan's phrase "with my heifer plow" is an allusion to Judges 14:18: "...And he [Samson] said unto them, If ye had not plowed with my heifer, ye had not found out my riddle." Bunyan also alludes to the Samson story, always a favorite with him, in the main work when the captains, hearing of Pry-well's report, "like so many Samsons ... shake themselves, and come together to consult and contrive how to defeat those bold and hellish contrivances that were upon the wheel, by the means of Diabolus and his friends...."[27] Referring to Psalm 81:16, he speaks of Emmanuel at his feast serving *honey* "out of the *rock*." The rock is a type of Christ, and God's bringing water from the rock for His people and from the jawbone for Samson becomes types of the deliverance to be wrought by Christ. In *The Holy War,* Emmanuel delivers answers to the riddles of Scripture and points out the rock to the Mansoulians. Bunyan thus brings "new honey" to Christ's way with Scripture by making his method in *The Holy War,* as foreshadowed in the two poems (the Address and the Adver-tisement to the Reader), mirror that approach. These addresses to the reader describe how to approach his work and actually set an example of approach through the allusions to the Samson story.

The Holy War is also "new honey" from John Bunyan in the sense that it extends the process defined in the preface of *Grace Abounding:* "I have sent you here enclosed a drop of that honey, that I have taken out of the Carcase of a Lyon (Judg. 14.5,6,7,8). I have eaten thereof my self also, and am much refreshed thereby. (Temptations when we meet them at first, are as the Lyon that roared upon Sampson; but if we over come them, the next time we see them, we shall finde a Nest of Honey within them.) The Philis-tians understand me not." Again, Bunyan's artistic sense is surpris-ingly sophisticated.

One of the most remarkable features of *The Holy War* is its extraordinary stress on the aural and, to a far lesser extent, visual senses. This use is, of course, quite in keeping with the Puritan view of calling or awakening and with Bunyan's own pictures of spiritual arousal by preaching, of which there are many examples in the present work; but the emphasis here is overwhelming and certainly deserves the critics' attention. The presence of the faculties in *Grace Abounding* and *The Pilgrim's Progress* is muted in comparison. To begin with, there are an amazing number of references to *seeing* and *hearing* in Bunyan's Address to the Reader, which along with the sequence on Samson's riddle, serves as a kind of ideograph to indicate not only *what* the reader can expect but *how* he can himself be made as receptive as possible to the messages of *The Holy War.*

In the allegory proper, both sides know the value of Ear-gate; they test it first and break through. The mayor appointed by Diabolus is earless and eyeless. Seldom is attention paid to other senses: Diabolus appoints special captains, Cruel and Torment, over Feel-gate; and Mansoul manages to get messages to Shaddai through Mouth-gate, probably an anticipation of the emphasis on Christiana and her followers *asking* for help in *The Pilgrim's Progress,* Part II. One can look to Bunyan's Puritan background for the primacy of God's calling through the aural sense; one can point out Puritan Milton's interpretation of obedience by its root meaning of "right hearing"; and one can cite Revelation's emphasis on "those who have ears," a strain often echoed in Bunyan's prefaces. The reader is still unprepared, however, for the great attention that the "ear of faith" receives in *The Holy War.* Like other devices and techniques of the work, focusing on the senses and on the faculties at large helps to turn what could have been a formal allegory into a homely account of what this battle has to do with every individual.

V   *Assets and Debits*

The Holy War deserves more attention and study. It often suffers from overcleverness; but it also bears marks of a careful writer when, for example, Bunyan demonstrates his emphasis on the inner man by structurally moving his audience, in the opening, downward through universe, town, and, finally, to Heart-Castle. He also conveys a sense of peaceful summers and long, hard winters and thereby prevents the work from floundering hopelessly in abstract and sometimes overly entangled theology.

As has been shown, this narrative is not without its flaws — its mixing of styles and its confusing of the multiple strands of the allegory. It also has its prejudices, however conventional they may be. Diabolus is made out to be king of the blacks or Negroes; and three of the children of Vile-affection and Carnal-lust — Impudence, Black-mouth, and Hate-reproof — are blacks. The remaining children — Scorn-truth, Slight-God, and Revenge — are females. Overall, women get little attention in *The Holy War*. The town might well be entirely male except that Bunyan indicates how the females will be molested by the Diabolonians.

Apart from these difficulties, Bunyan's allegory is a long and sometimes tedious work. Just as the reader thinks that it has gone totally arid, however, he arrives at one of those droll Bunyanesque moments when Carnal-security asks Godly-fear if he is afraid of being "sparrow-blasted," when old Diabolus "snuff[s] up the wind like a dragon," or when the narrator reports that Ill-pause is wounded and that "some say" his "brain-pan" is cracked. The reader continues to read.

CHAPTER 6

Part II of
The Pilgrim's Progress

I *The Pilgrimage*

I N Part II of *The Pilgrim's Progress* (1684), Bunyan returns to a
narrated allegory of life as a pilgrimage and presents Christian's
family on the road to salvation. The "narrator" informs his
audience that, though he has been too busy to tell this story before,
his concerns have recently brought him in the vicinity of the events
about to be unfolded. As the narrator sleeps and dreams, he meets
and walks with Mr. Sagacity, who tells him that the "Prince"
(Christ) is coming to check on those of the City of Destruction who
laughed at Christian. The old man next promises to tell the narrator
about Christian's wife, now called "Christiana" because she has
become a pilgrim, and about their four boys, all of whom have
taken Christian's route.

Christiana thinks of her husband and is sorry that she blamed his
despair on his fancy and on melancholy. As she sleeps, her dream-
within-the-dream consists of three scenes: she sees a parchment
with her sins and cries out for mercy; two "ill-favored ones"
speculate on their fear that she will follow Christian; and she sees
Christian in heaven, where he and his companions can understand
the words of the angels. The following morning, Secret comes to
invite her to go to the Wicket-gate with a letter from her husband's
King in her bosom. When Mrs. Timorous and Mercy visit
Christiana, they immediately recognize a change in her and in her
language, for she is one of "God's chosen." The plan to travel
after Christian appears ridiculous to Timorous; but Mercy yearns to
accompany Christiana, who offers to hire her as a servant and to inter-
cede for her at the Wicket-gate. mercy weeps for those left behind;
and the company, including the sons of Christiana, starts out.

The Slough of Despond is worse now than in Christian's time, but Mercy's boldness sets the band to the venture. At the Wicket-gate, they knock but are frightened by a dog. The Keeper answers and has a trumpeter entertain for their benefit, but Mercy is left outside. True to her promise, Christiana begs acceptance for Mercy, who knocks again but then succumbs to a swoon and has to be revived with myrrh. The visitors are next taken up to the wall to be shown how they are saved; and then Mercy and Christiana, left in the summer-parlor, fall to talking. Before they leave this place to travel on, Mercy remonstrates about the dog.

As they go along the way, on the other side of the wall is the Devil's garden, and the boys eat of the fruit that hangs over this wall toward them. Two ill-favored strangers approach and lay violent hands on the women; but the ladies are eventually saved by the Reliever, who rebukes them for not having requested a guide. Christiana also realizes that she has been warned of this attack in her dream.

Approaching the House of the Interpreter, the group hears Christiana's name mentioned, and Innocence answers their knock. The visitors are taken to the Significant Rooms, where they see the man in the iron cage, the man who dreams of Judgment, the man who fights his way through his enemies, and the picture of the great man. Then they are shown the Muckraker, a spider on the wall of the best room, a hen and her chicks, a slaughterhouse, a garden with a great variety of flowers, a field of straw, a robin with a spider, and a tree rotten on the inside. During dinner, they are entertained with music, and then both women tell their stories to the Interpreter. In bed afterward, Mercy cannot sleep for happiness. The next morning, the travelers are bathed, dressed in white linen, and sealed with the Interpreter's mark. The Interpreter sends his servant Great-heart, with his sword, helmet, and shield, to conduct them; and they go singing on their way.

At the place where Christian lost his burden, they pause to praise God, while Great-heart discourses on Christ's pardon and ransom. Passing on, they see Simple, Sloth, and Presumption hanged and hear of those persuaded to turn out of the way as a result of their bad report of God. They find the springs of the Hill of Difficulty dirty now and have to wait for the dregs of the waters to sink. Great-heart points out the byways taken by Formality and Hypocrisy; and they climb on until they reach an arbor, where they halt to refresh themselves. When Christiana leaves behind a bottle of

"spirits" in this "losing place," she has to send one of the boys
back to fetch it.

They soon come upon a stage bearing a description of the punishment of Timorous and Mistrust, who tried to turn Christian
back with fear of the lions. Now the Giant Grim backs the lions,
but he is killed by Great-heart. At the Porter's Lodge, Great-heart
must leave them, since the pilgrims have failed to ask the Master
for the help of their guide beyond this point. The Porter Watchful
asks Christiana's story, while Humble-mind and others of this
place make plans for dinner. Afterward, Christiana and Mercy
retire to their chamber to talk; and Christiana later hears her companion laugh in her sleep. The next morning, Mercy tells of her
dream: she was bemoaning her "hardness of heart" when a
"shining one" took her to heaven. The visitors stay here about a
month in order to come to know Prudence, Piety, and Charity, the
last of whom catechizes the children. During this period, Mercy's
busy ways of making hose and garments attract a suitor, Mr. Brisk;
but he ceases his courtship when he finds that she gets no money by
her occupation.

Also at the Palace Beautiful, Matthew, one of Christiana's sons,
has a bout of the "gripes" from eating the green plums of Beelzebub's orchard. Doctor Skill's first purge — goat blood, the ashes of
a heifer, and the juice of hyssop — is ineffective. Then he applies a
dose *ex Carne* and *sanguine Christi,* "from the body and blood of
Christ," and the child is healed. Later, Matthew asks Prudence a
series of edifying questions; and Joseph reminds his mother, Christiana, to send the Interpreter a request for the services of Great-
heart. The pilgrims are then shown a series of things on which to
meditate as they travel: one of the apples of Eve, Jacob's ladder, a
golden anchor, and the mountain where Abraham offered Isaac.
Prudence plays the virginals and sings for them. Great-heart arrives
with wine and food. The Porter gives them news of the highway,
blesses them, and receives a "gold angel" from Christiana. They
are about to depart when Piety remembers something she has
meant to give Christiana. While they wait for Piety's return, Prudence tells them about the birds they hear singing in a grove. Piety
provides Christiana with a "scheme" of the emblems they have
seen at the Palace Beautiful, and they resume their journey.

In the Valley of Humiliation, they find a pillar describing Christian's "slips" as he came downhill. They pass a boy feeding his
father's sheep and hear his song. They see mementos of the battle

between Christian and Apollyon, and Mercy especially feels a kindredship with this valley. But, when the travelers reach the Valley of the Shadow of Death, it is uncomfortable for all. They hear groans and hisses and feel the ground shake beneath them. Christiana's son James becomes sick with fear and has to be administered some of the pills his mother has received from Doctor Skill. Although they see a fiend and then a lion, they are not accosted. Mist and darkness issue from a pit; they pray, are beset with horrible odors and with snares, and observe Heedless at the bottom of a ditch on their left. Eventually, they come to the cave of the Giant Maul, the sophist, who accuses God's ministers of the crime of kidnapping. Great-heart slays this creature, and they set up a pillar with an account of their adventures and with the giant's head as warnings for others who might follow them in the way. Then they rest on the spot where Christian first saw Faithful.

Under an oak, they find an old pilgrim, Honest, asleep. He is reluctant to give his name and blushes when Great-heart recognizes him. At the request of Honest, Great-heart tells of the adventures of Fearing, who, being troubled by nothing physical, but only by a fear of his not being accepted by God at the last, found great sympathy in the Valley of Humiliation. Like the present pilgrims, however, he had great difficulties in the Valley of the Shadow of Death and was more afflicted by it than even James was. Strangely, the water of the river was at its lowest when Fearing passed over. Mercy and Christiana both express a feeling of spiritual likeness to this Fearing. Honest responds with the story of Mr. Selfwil, who thought that he could with impunity commit the sins of the saints. Christiana laments for those who do not repent until they are dying.

A figure warns the pilgrims of robbers, but they safely reach the inn of Gaius, who gives instructions for their entertainment, talks of Christian's ancestors, warns Christiana to get her children married so as to insure that her husband's name will be carried on, and speaks on behalf of women. After dinner, the adults sit up all night talking and telling riddles and anecdotes. During their stay, Gaius, Great-heart, and Honest attack Slay-good; and Great-heart cuts off that giant's head. They rescue Feeble-mind, the nephew of Fearing, and hear his story, as well as that of the death of Not-Right from thunder. Matthew marries Mercy; James marries Phoebe, the daughter of Gaius; and they are all feasted. The pilgrims remain with Gaius over ten days after the weddings and are joined when they leave by Mr. Ready-to-halt.

Great-heart talks about Christian as the pilgrims go along the route. They next arrive at Vanity Fair in the evening and stay with old Mnason, who sends his daughter Grace to invite the other good men in this town to meet his guests. The pilgrims learn that persecution has lessened here. Grace marries Samuel; and another of Mnason's daughters, Martha, marries Joseph. While the group is staying in Vanity Fair, a monster makes one of his seasonal attacks on the town to steal its children; but he is so lamed by the defenders that he probably will die.

After leaving Vanity Fair, the pilgrims pass the Hill Lucre and come to the river before the Delectable Mountains. They find a man in whose care they can leave Christiana's grandchildren. The men of the party march on Doubting Castle, kill the Giantess Diffidence, and cut off the head of her husband, Despair. Music and dancing celebrate this victory and the subsequent freeing of Despondency and his daughter, Much-afraid. They now pass on to the Delectable Mountains, where the shepherds show them the sights Christian saw, plus new scenes on Mounts Marvel, Innocent, and Charity, as well as Fool and Want-wit trying unsuccessfully to wash an Ethiopian white. Mercy asks to see the hole in the side of the hill that marks the byway to hell. She is pregnant and yearns for a looking glass hanging in the shepherds' dining room. When Christiana reveals this desire, the shepherds praise Mercy for it and quickly give her the mirror. As the singing pilgrims leave, they pass the places where Christian met Turn-away and where Little-Faith was robbed. When they meet Valiant-for-truth, who has a bloody face and a drawn sword, they hear about this character's being attacked by Wild-head, Inconsiderate, and Pragmatic and about his being drawn to a pilgrimage by learning the story of Christian.

In the Enchanted Ground, the pilgrims encounter so much mist and such intense darkness that they are forced to feel their way along. They pass the first arbor, the friend of the slothful, without stopping. The way is difficult, and Great-heart takes out a map (the Bible?). In the second arbor, they find Heedless and Too-bold talking in their sleep but cannot awaken them. The children cry for help, and a wind drives off the fog. They go on and meet a man on his knees, who turns out to be Mr. Stand-fast and who is in the stance of prayer to ward off more attacks from Mrs. Bubble.

At last, Beulah, the land of their "marriage with Christ," receives them with trumpets, bells, and nosegays; and they find that here they do not need sleep. Messengers of Death come, in turn, to Christiana, Ready-to-halt, Feeble-mind, Despondency, Honest, Valiant-for-truth, and Stand-fast. Much-afraid requests to be allowed to accompany her father, Despondency. Each of those who have received a message also receives a token and delivers some final words before he or she crosses the river. The narrator does not wait to see Christiana's children and grandchildren called; but he promises, if he passes this way again, to give an account of that about which he is now silent.

II   *The Meaning of the Allegory*

Part II of *The Pilgrim's Progress* continues to allegorize the process of conversion dealt with in Part I, but the differences between the sequel and the parent work quickly become apparent. Although Bunyan continues to alternate action and contemplation, the rites of conversion have become open to individuals vastly unlike Christian or the Bunyan pictured in *Grace Abounding*. Dissenters in England at this time enjoyed diminished persecution, and Bunyan's church had flourished. He himself was ministering to congregations throughout the area of Bedford and Elstow, as well as preaching on occasion in London. With the growth of membership came a diversification of spiritual needs, and Bunyan tries to speak to as many of them as possible in *The Pilgrim's Progress,* Part II. He of necessity becomes less personal and less intimate as he moves to religious experiences for the most part unlike his own. Conviction of sin had, after all, occupied a long period of his conversion.

The long discourses of Part I are greatly reduced in the story of the women and the children; but Great-heart does descant at the Cross on pardon, ransom, and the godhead and manhood of Christ. Much of the "doctrine" is carried dramatically, as in the case of the *general* versus the *special* calling to salvation dealt with in Mercy's fears, in Christiana's promises to her, and in the "fourfold" interpretation of the hen and chicks at the Interpreter's House. Like Christian before her, Christiana has received God's special call; but Mercy has no proof of such treatment and enters the Wicket-gate by right of the gift that Christ's sacrifice has made available to all. "Sanctification," one of the late phases of conversion, is demonstrated by the bath in the Interpreter's House, by the "sealing" (the mark of the redeemed in Revelation), and by being dressed in white linen. That bath also symbolizes the Baptist rite of

immersion and is a little too similar to the Apocryphal story of
Susanna and the elders and to the biblical story of Bathsheba on the
roof to assert its full allegorical function. As Henri Talon suggests,
Bunyan shows that adult baptism is, if not absolutely necessary, at
least salutary; and he has thus made a concession to the strict Baptists with whom he was constantly at odds.[1]

At the Palace Beautiful, Doctor Skill's first purge symbolizes the
sacrifices under the Law and is consequently ineffective. When he
applies a dose made from the body and blood of Christ, healing
takes place. Bunyan has in one quick instance moved from moral
conversion to the centrality of Christ's sacrifice in the experience of
every individual.

The terror of hardness of the heart that is so strong in *Grace
Abounding* is present in Part II of *The Pilgrim's Progress* through
the softening veil of a dream and is overcome therein as Mercy
laughs in her sleep. An emphasis on suffering and patience comes
in the tableau of the quiet sheep in the House of the Interpreter.
The women and children do not see the blood of the crucified
Christ or the holes of the nails in the body; rather, from the top of
the Wicket-gate, they view the Crucifixion "afar off." The pilgrims
also find that a righteous fear is not unacceptable to God. A significant change from Part I and from *Grace Abounding*, in which,
even in the late stages of conversion, the candidate suffered
periodic dosages of despair, arrives with the slaying of the Giant
Despair.

Overall, the emphasis is on the mutual benefits of shared religious experiences. Bunyan continues to display the whole and the
typical curve of Puritan concern; for, once individual conversion
has been accomplished, the tendency is to look outward to all members of the religious community. Thus, the parts of the conversion
process stressed in Part II of *The Pilgrim's Progress* are those that
are more communal: calling, justification through faith, sanctification in the godly life, and glorification, and particularly the last
two. Little is made here of conviction of sin or of the soul-
rendering seizures of despair that one is among the elect.

III *Flaws*

Critics generally concede that Part I of *The Pilgrim's Progress* is
better than Part II, and the two are often contrasted along such
lines as "Bunyan the Puritan" versus "Bunyan the Humanist" or

"epic" versus "romance." Part II does seem rather clumsy at times, as the following examples illustrate. Great-heart at one point refers to himself in the third person as though he were not the speaker. Although all of the children eat the Devil's *fruit,* only Matthew is identified later in the work as culpable; and he is then said to have eaten *green plums.* In Part I, Christian and Hopeful are punished for crossing into By-path Meadow; here, though the warriors of the group discuss the possible consequences of taking detours, they deliberately leave the path to assault Doubting Castle. Ironically, *Tell-true* has helped to convert Valiant-for-truth by describing the adventures of Christian, such as the killing of a "serpent"; but, unless he is referring to Apollyon, this episode does not occur in Part I.

The transitions from one event to another during the course of the occasionally long stops at the various resting places are so often forced that Bunyan appears to be writing with some haste. Thus there is an abrupt shift from Brisk's courtship of Mercy to Matthew's sickness to the questions Matthew sets Prudence and to the revelation that the month at the House Beautiful, not named as such in Part II, has ended. Then there is the awkward way in which the information about the wedding of Mercy and Matthew is set forth. After Gaius insists that Christian's name must not be allowed to die, Bunyan announces this alliance, adding, "But more of that hereafter." He proceeds to repeat the news twice more, after having finally achieved satisfaction by marrying all of the sons and then forgetting to strike the references to Matthew alone. Equally strange is the fact that the original frame of a dialogue between the narrator and Sagacity is dropped after the Slough of Despond episode: "And now Mr. *Sagacity* left me to Dream out my Dream by my self." Since Bunyan had successfully used the dialogue in *Badman,* the reader can only conclude that he was careless in not excising it here after he returned to the narrative mode of Part I.

The narrator himself is less visible in this part and seems much more detached and genial, as he casually intimates that he might some day continue the family's adventures on the road. He could easily be extracted from the ending of Part II; but removing him from the fortunes of Christian, Hopeful, and Ignorance would mar their ending irreparably. He there acts as a mediator of the experience for the audience, but the tale of Christiana does not seem to move him equally. The ending of Part II is a purple passage that is extremely beautiful in its own right; for, in the words of Roger

Sharrock, "The summons to each pilgrim follows an impressively regular formula, so that the whole final episode has a marked rhythm, an almost musical pattern of recurrence and variation. There is the letter from the Celestial City, the emblematic token of its authenticity, the bequest of each one before crossing the river, and their last words. The use throughout of the imagery of death from Ecclesiastes xii was habitual at Puritan deathbeds...."[2] From the very patterning of this finale, however, one infers a detachment on the part of the narrator, who may not be capable of full empathy with the females, children, feeble, and simple of the later work. Bunyan's own spiritual fight had, after all, been like that of Christian.

Bunyan seems a conscious craftsman as he makes us forget the more poignant ending of Part I by first setting up the pattern of the deaths and then by breaking that pattern on two counts: Christiana does not say anything to Stand-fast but simply gives him a ring; Much-afraid belies her name by determining to accompany her father without having been officially called to die.

IV   Relations between Parts I and II

Euphemism and indirection to some degree obstructed the fact of death in Part I of *The Pilgrim's Progress;* but in Part II, Christiana talks to her sons about the *death* of their father. Christian in fact becomes for the new pilgrims an emblem or symbol of the Right Professor's journey to heaven. In a classic manner, he set his pattern in Christ in keeping with the Puritan doctrine specifically developed by Bunyan in *Of Justification By An Imputed Righteousness; Or, No way to Heaven but by Jesus Christ* (first printed in 1692). Now Christian is the type for additional pilgrims to follow. This is beautifully illustrated by the fact that, while he is treated to the pedigree of Christ in the Palace Beautiful, Christiana hears from Gaius the ancestry of her own husband.

Christian is a dominating figure in Part II, then; and Bunyan becomes rather Miltonic in using him as a mediator between Christ and others, as Adam is a mediator between Eve and God in *Paradise Lost.* Yet Bunyan is sufficiently realistic to allow the new pilgrims to profit from Christian's mistakes. He may be an emblem, but he is not perfect. There are rumors afoot that he lost faith and drowned in crossing the river, and the Christiana cortege reads of his "slips" during the descent to the Valley of Humiliation.

Besides the established route of the journey and the example of Christian, there are many interconnections between the two parts — and enough variations to make the sequel entertaining in and of itself. Just as "Graceless" became "Christian," Christiana receives her name with her assumption of the status of a pilgrim. Bunyan places more emphasis than formerly on the Puritan "community of believers"; everyone wants to hear the adventures of Christiana and the others. The exemplary function of the whole of Part I is reinforced by the appearance in Part II of the son of Great-grace in the emblem picture of Mount Marvel, as well as by the conversion of so many of the episodes of the first journey into emblemlike monuments to be meditated on by Christiana's group. Bunyan drives home ever more vividly the correlation between the topography of the route and the state of mind of the individual pilgrim. In a long account, Great-heart establishes the deep empathy of "chicken-hearted" Fearing with the Valley of Humiliation; and Mercy, too, finds herself inclining to its spirit. The reader is reminded that the Lord of the Hill (Christ) was once there and that humiliation and persecution are the lot of the faithful.

The arrows of the Devil, a great danger in Part I, become a dog (the Devil in disguise), an example of Bunyan's accommodating to the more domestic fears of the females and the children. Faithful's experience with Wanton is relived in that of Stand-fast with Bubble; but, at the same time, an explanation is provided for Demas, whom the good madam has seduced. Help is paralleled by the Reliever of Part II, and Mrs. Timorous is as much afraid to venture with Christiana as her husband was of the lions in the way. Valiant-for-truth may originate in Faithful's remark in Part I: *"I think we must cry to him for help against shame, that would have us be valiant for Truth upon the Earth."*[3] Similarly, Honest's refusing to tell his name recalls By-ends' stalling in delivering his in Part I and becomes a way of distinguishing two moral types as well as of indicating that By-ends is human enough to be ashamed of his reputation. Honest and one of Christiana's sons, like certain characters of Part I, show their own humanity by blushing.

Some of the minor characters speak with the literal-mindedness of their predecessors: Mrs. Timorous says, "...while we are out of danger we are out; but when we are in, we are in."[4] Bunyan frequently displays his earlier ability to depict a minor character by a ticket-name, for "Taste-that-which-is-good" highlights Gaius' cook and the cuisine at the inn where Christiana and her party

wisely loiter. The speaking accents of a character are captured even
through the distance of another's description, as Honest asks of
Madam Bubble: *"Doth she not speak very smoothly, and give you
a Smile at the end of a Sentence?"*[5]

Occasionally, too, Bunyan returns to Part I's intrusion of allegorical vehicle, here demonstrated by Christiana's pronouncement
in the Grim episode: "...tho' the Travellers have been made in
time past, to walk thorough by-Paths, it must not be so now I am
risen, *Now I am Risen a Mother in Israel."*[6] At such moments, the
literal and the figurative become entangled; and Bunyan makes
Henry Peacham's working definition of allegory as "one thing in
words, another in sense" go awry.

V   *General Atmosphere and Techniques*

The atmosphere of The Pilgrim's Progress, Part II, is, as is generally agreed, lighter and more pleasing, with a frequent mention of
"sunshine days." The ladies have male guides and protectors, but
there are some fearful moments: they are almost sexually assaulted[7]
— despite their highly reasonable precaution of putting down their
veils! — and the Valley of the Shadow of Death is approximately as
difficult for this party as it was for Christian. On the other hand,
their "conviction of sin" is hardly noticed, in contrast with Christian's burden; and, although the Slough of Despond is far worse,
they manage it easily. The spring of the Hill of Difficulty is dirty
now, but the episode of Vanity Fair becomes a long and pleasant
visit with Mnason. There is no Hill of the Law threatening to fall
on their heads, and Mercy *must ask* to see the hole to hell in the side
of the hill. They receive frequent warnings of robbers and mis-
creants, but none materializes.

As has often been noted, the pace is more leisurely in Part II.
Christian and Hopeful spend several days at the river bank of the
medicinal trees, but Christiana and her companions pass over a
month at the House Beautiful alone. Hospitality receives even more
stress in Part II, and Gaius and Mnason are selected by Bunyan for
their connection with the New Testament's entertainment of the
disciples. There is, indeed, much feasting throughout. The atmosphere of "eat, drink, and be merry" prevails at the wedding celebration; and one of the minor ironies is that the completion of that
verse — "for tomorrow you may *die*" — is also apropos.

Christian is a mature family man through his entire story. Christiana and her children age en route, with Gaius speaking of the heroine as an "aged matron" to Mercy's "young damsel." Matthew's aging seems to follow a geometrical progression, for he is apparently a child in the opening and gains the years necessary to become Mercy's husband. In fact, one gets the impression that Mercy was actually engaged by Christiana as a kind of baby-sitter for her future husband. Moreover, Christiana's promise to her that they will "hold all things in common" comes literally true in the case of Matthew, to the delight of the audience.

Homely touches of Part I are expanded here, as in Christiana's request at the House Beautiful to sleep in her husband's chamber, Mercy's remonstrations with the Keeper about the dog, the discontinuation of Brisk's courtship when he learns that Mercy will not charge for her wares, and the halt Stand-fast makes in the middle of the river to chat with those left on the shore. The spiritual kinship between the uncle, Fearing, and the nephew, Feeblemind, is reinforced by the physical traits of the family: *"...you have his whitely Look, a Cast like his with your Eye, and your Speech is much alike."*[8] Nor has Bunyan, despite some carelessness, lost his love of detail. On the Hill of Difficulty, Christiana is able to offer the others refreshments that are accounted for by having Mercy suddenly recall that the Interpreter took Christiana aside and gave her something for the trip. Great-heart just happens to have a tinderbox along so that he can strike a light to read his map by in the darkness of the Enchanted Ground.

Part II also has dreams-within-the-dream, and Bunyan's justification of "sleep-work" has evoked psychological interpretations of both parts. Christiana's dreams convince her of her sin, warn her of future dangers, and sustain her with a vision of Christian in heaven. Mercy's fears are quelled by the dream that she will be allowed to enter God's presence, and Christiana adapts Job to assure her that she need feel no guilt for dreaming: "God speaks once, yea twice, yet man perceiveth it not. In a Dream, in a Vision of the Night, when deep sleep falleth upon men, in slumbering upon the Bed. *We need not, when a-Bed, lie awake to talk with God; he can visit us while we sleep, and cause us then to hear his Voice. Our Heart oft times wakes when we sleep, and God can speak to that, either by Words, by Proverbs, by Signs, and Similitudes, as well as if one was awake.*"[9] This passage forms one of the most beautiful moments in a work where such moments abound, and it also calls to mind Adam's description in *Paradise Lost* of what happens while he and Eve sleep.

In Part II, Bunyan's proverbs appear most often in the songs and poems, which are more frequent than in Part I. Christiana is certain that "'Tis better late than never," and the pilgrims also set the proverb to moral use in "Some tho they shun the Frying-pan, / Do leap into the Fire." The shepherd boy's lovely lyric, one of the most famous in *The Pilgrim's Progress,* is also aphoristic: "He that is down, need fear no fall, / He that is low, no Pride...." As is customary with Bunyan, then, even his standard and traditional materials are not merely ornamental; for example, a great point is made with regard to Christiana's spiritual acquiescence by the fact that she repeats Secret's "bitter before the sweet" to Mrs. Timorous.

Puns, double entendres, and quibbles abound from the opening, as Christiana cries out for "mercy" in her sleep and gets that and "Mercy," too. Bunyan mixes doctrine, humor, and domesticity as "the lamb [Christ] with the accustomed sauce" is prepared for the pilgrims. A standard Renaissance pun is used when Christiana tips the Porter a "gold angel." The arbor on the Hill of Difficulty is a "losing place" not only for those too lazy to try to climb the way and who thus "lose" heaven, but also for Christian's pardon and Christiana's bottle of "spirits." Bunyan is rather brutal in the ticket-name he assigns to Mrs. "Bat's Eyes"; but, when she insists that Christiana is "blind," she fails to recognize that she herself is spiritually "blind as a bat." Given the company she keeps — Mesdames Light-mind, Love-the-flesh, Wanton, and Filth — she may also "bat her eyes" in flirtation. Feeble-mind has the presence of mind to request that his friends bury his feeble mind in a dunghill, and Valiant-for-truth fights with a "right Jerusalem blade." But surely Mercy's pun is unintended when, at the end of the mirror episode, she says to the shepherds: "By this I know that I have obtained *Favour* in your Eyes."[10]

Musical references are more numerous in Part II. The Keeper of the Gate has a trumpeter entertain the arriving pilgrims, and the Interpreter has minstrels provide dinner music. Mercy and Christiana hear a "noise" of music for joy that they have arrived safely at the Porter's Lodge. Prudence plays a "pair of virginals" while Christiana and Mercy, after the downfall of Despair, play the viol and the lute, respectively. Even Ready-to-halt, though he is "ready-to-halt" and has to use one of his crutches, leads Much-afraid in a dance. Birds sing for joy in the grove, and bells and trumpets sound throughout Beulah. Of special import is Bunyan's use of the bass and sackbut as metaphors, that use being justified, as Great-heart explains, by Revelation's comparison of the saved to a company of musicians:

Some must *Pipe,* and some must *Weep:* Now Mr. *Fearing* was one that play'd upon *this Base.* He and his fellows sound the *Sackbut,* whose Notes are more doleful than the Notes of other Musick are. Tho indeed some say, the Base is the ground [a pun?] of Musick. And for my part, I care not at all for that Profession that begins not in heaviness of Mind. The first string that the Musitian usually touches, *is the Base,* when he intends to put all in tune; God also plays upon this string first, when he sets the Soul in tune for himself. Only here was the imperfection of Mr. *Fearing,* he could play upon no other Musick but this, till towards his latter end.[11]

Bunyan's purple passage is the domesticated version of the music of the spheres and of John Donne's "I tune the instrument here at the door."

Part II of *The Pilgrim's Progress* seems to promote church music and refers to metrical versions of the Psalms. Bunyan's *A Treatise of the Fear of God* (1679) includes a singing version of Psalm 128; and it seems likely that Bunyan, unlike the more conservative Baptists, encouraged singing and music in public worship. As many critics have suggested, he may have been propagandizing for a return to some of the more emotional features of religion. At the least, he evinces a "Humanistic Puritanism" and aligns himself thereby with Milton and Cromwell, both of whom, though Puritans themselves, disapproved of the Puritan destruction of the great church organs and of the subsequent quiescence of complex and beautiful church music.

As in Part I, songs or poems serve chiefly to give spiritual point to episodes, to provide transitions, or to form interludes between adventures. They sometimes become almost miniatures of the episodes in a way similar to Christiana's "scheme" of the journey. Accordingly, they reinforce the sacramental and emblematic atmosphere already in evidence through the monuments to the events of Part I. Just as that first part becomes exemplary for the characters of the second, the second part is in the process of becoming exemplary for the audience with the passage of its events into the moral postscripts of the songs and the poems.

On the other hand, the songs and poems may be simply refreshing changes of pace performed by someone who is outside the group of pilgrims. For example, the shepherd boy's song in the Valley of Humiliation is one of Bunyan's few good poems and is the only one to be included in *The Oxford Book of English Verse:*

> *He that is down, needs fear no fall,*
> *He that is low, no Pride:*
> *He that is humble, ever shall*
> *Have God to be his Guide.*
>
> *I am content with what I have,*
> *Little be it, or much:*
> *And, Lord, Contentment still I crave,*
> *Because thou savest such.*
>
> *Fulness to such a burden is*
> *That go on Pilgrimage:*
> *Here little, and hereafter Bliss,*
> *Is best from Age to Age.*[12]

It is ironic that, as several have noticed, the first lines are similar to these of Samuel Butler's satire of the Puritans, *Hudibras:* "I am not now in Fortune's power. / He that is down can fall no lower."

Bunyan's other outstanding poem is Valiant-for-truth's "Who would true Valour see," which is often compared with Amiens' song in Shakespeare's *As You Like It* (act 2, scene 5) and which was used in the funeral service of Sir Winston Churchill. Mackail feels that this poem is Bunyan's one success in capturing the authentic note of Elizabethan England's great lyric period and suggests that it was meant to be sung to the tune of the popular "Phyllida flouts me."[13] Here it is:

> *Who would true Valour see*
> *Let him come hither;*
> *One here will Constant be,*
> *Come Wind, come Weather.*
> *There's no* Discouragement,
> *Shall make him once* Relent,
> *His first avow'd* Intent,
> *To be a Pilgrim.*
>
> *Who so beset him round,*
> *With dismal* Storys,
> *Do but themselves Confound;*
> *His strength the* more is.
> *No* Lyon *can him fright,*
> *He'l with a* Gyant *Fight,*
> *But he will have a right,*
> *To be a Pilgrim.*

> Hobgoblin, *nor foul* Fiend,
> *Can* daunt *his Spirit:*
> *He knows, he* at the end,
> Shall Life Inherit.
> *Then Fancies fly away,*
> *He'l fear not what men say,*
> *He'l labour Night and Day,*
> To be a Pilgrim.[14]

Bunyan's fondness for riddles and his feeling that obscure and dark texts allure the mind are stressed anew in the preface to Part II. And in the work proper, Gaius' "poem" follows the same line of thought; and its analogy is reminiscent of patristic exegesis:

> *Hard* Texts *are* Nuts (I *will not call them* Cheaters,)
> *Whose* Shells *do keep their* Kirnels *from the Eaters.*
> *Ope then the Shells, and you shall have the Meat,*
> *They here are brought, for you to crack and eat.*

This same view of Scripture is put forth in his earlier works and is elaborated on by the presentation of emblems[15] in the House of the Interpreter.

The pilgrims also entertain one another with riddles in a way that recalls the delight of Emmanuel's guests with his clarification of the "old texts" in *The Holy War.* Bunyan displays increasing sophistication in the use of riddles, for they are several times combined with other forms. The spider in the Interpreter's House, for example, blends riddle and emblem. The questions that Matthew puts to Prudence are quite an advance over the catechism Bunyan had used in *Instruction for the Ignorant* (1675), for they merge riddle, emblem, and catechism; for example, "'*Why do the Springs come from the Sea to us, thorough the Earth?*' 'To shew that the Grace of God comes to us thorough the Body of Christ.'" To the Renaissance generally, this quotation would suggest the emblem and metaphor of the conduits of God. Gaius' "story" of youth and age is really a riddle that illustrates the appropriateness of the companionship of the "matron" Christiana and her youthful band and their mutually supportive functions.

Perhaps because of the more relaxed atmosphere of Part II, there are fewer exclamations, such as "Huh," for expended effort; but there are still amusing Bunyan colloquialisms. To the dismay of early editors, Bunyan borrows from the jargon of cockfighting in

Great-heart's description of Valiant-for-truth as a "Cock of the right kind." With a proven capacity for painting word-pictures, Bunyan allows Christiana to assess Difficulty as a "breathing Hill." The Interpreter leavens his emblems with an interlude of thirteen spiritually pointed "maxims," such as "He that lives in Sin, and looks for Happiness hereafter, is like him that soweth Cockle, and thinks to fill his Barn with Wheat, or Barley" or "If a man would live well, let him fetch his last day to him, and make it always his company-Keeper." As these quotations demonstrate, Bunyan's forte is the blending of the Bible with aphorisms and seventeenth-century idioms. There are also a few references in this work to classical and nonbiblical figures, such as Ignatius, Hercules, and Romanus.

Giants have multiplied now that there are adequate numbers of "Davids" or "Jacks" to dispatch them for the ladies. Grim or Bloody Man, who backs the lions, is a combination of Bloodybones of folklore, the Bloodmen of *The Holy War,* and the religious persecutors of all persuasions. Maul and his sophistry again rally the hue and cry after the Jesuits, who had assumed new prominence with the Popish Plot (1678). But it is also interesting that *maul* is a favorite word with Bunyan and is frequently used in connection with the Diabolonians of *The Holy War.* Slay-good, the "seasonal" villain of Vanity Fair, and Despair and his wife Diffidence complete the parade of the giants for adventure-lovers. It is little wonder that a recent criticism of *The Pilgrim's Progress* appeared in the journal *Children's Literature* and treated it as a fairy tale.[16]

For ingenuity and daring within the allegorical framework, one is not likely to forget Matthew and the plums as the world's most *un*likely way to get at Original Sin. Mercy's swooning is also an unexpected ideograph for fear of being too late to receive Christ's pardon or of not having been called to election. Likewise, Mercy's longing for the mirror is an extraordinarily daring execution when the first reaction of the audience is to be amused at the age-old problems of the pregnant female, while the second is a puzzlement in view of the popular association of the mirror with vanity. For their bizarreness, the reader will not forget the Muckraker and the spider; for their beauty and touching simplicity, the Valley of Humiliation for Mercy and Fearing and the ending of Part II; or for the piquancy of a slight prurience, the attack of the "ill-favored ones" and Madam Bubble's attempted seduction of Stand-fast. In a work so thoroughly religious, the range of moods is indeed surprising.

There are references to the faculties, but they are of a more general nature than those of Part I. The term *fancy(ies)* occurs throughout and is connected with a right and wrong use of the imagination: right, when Bunyan speaks of the whole of Part II as his *fancies*; wrong, when a false pilgrim is blamed for following his "false" fancies. The senses themselves are treated rather literally. The Valley of the Shadow of Death "stinks"; and in the Enchanted Ground, the pilgrims cannot see and must *feel* their way. As is customary in Bunyan's beatific portions, which draw upon the sensuousness of Canticles, all of the senses are catered to and cared for in Beulah and heaven, as in the revival of Mercy with myrrh and the nosegays from the King's Garden. The pilgrims feast their eyes on the objects of meditation in the Palace Beautiful. The emphasis on preaching and on reaching the inner ear is perpetuated in Valiant-for-truth's being persuaded to become a pilgrim by Tell-true; in Great-heart, another portrait of John Gifford; and in the Interpreter, who is also a kind of minister.

VI *Christian Fellowship and the Portrait of Women*

"Doctrinally," Bunyan, in what some have called an "after-piece," felt the need to examine Christian or church fellowship, as well as to combat the number of unauthentic sequels that had appeared. The continuation of Part I by the General Baptist T[homas] S[herman] had suggested a deficiency in the area of fellowship. Moreover, in *A Case of Conscience Resolved* (1683), Bunyan had rejected the request of the women in his congregation for a separate meeting. He may have wished to compensate for his refusal of this privilege and to offset the grim picture of Christian's family in Part I: "Why, my Wife was afraid of losing this World; and my Children were given to the foolish delights of youth...."[17] Charity compounds the affront to women by linking them with Cain: "*Indeed* Cain *hated his Brother, because his own works were evil, and his Brothers righteous; and if thy Wife and Children have been offended with thee for this, they thereby shew themselves to be implacable to good; and thou hast delivered thy soul from their blood.*"[18] No woman can forgive Christian's sticking his fingers in his ears and his running away to avoid his wife's conversation, no matter how often Christiana is read as the symbol of the fleshly

world or how beautiful the female figure appears elsewhere in
Part I in the damsel sprinkling water, who represents the Gospel,
and in Prudence, Charity, Discretion, and Piety.

Bunyan's doctrine again prevailed in Part II, and only by the
sheerest effort of willpower does he salvage the female by having
old Gaius speak for her. Even then, only an equipoise is struck:
against Eve, Gaius balances the mother of Jesus; but he does admit
that women were the first to rejoice in the Savior. Ultimately, the
Bible is called to witness:

I read not that ever any man did give unto Christ so much as one *Groat,*
but the Women followed him, and ministred to him of their Substance.
'Twas a Woman that washed his Feet with Tears, and a Woman that
anointed his Body to the Burial. They were Women that wept when he was
going to the Cross; And Women that followed him from the Cross, and
that sat by his Sepulcher when he was buried. They were Women that was
first with him at his Resurrection *morn,* and Women that brought Tidings
first to his Disciples that he was risen from the Dead. Women therefore are
highly favoured, and shew by these things that they are sharers with us in
the Grace of Life.[19]

Ironically, Bunyan's prose becomes almost incantatory as he
praises women in this purple passage.

For the rest of Part II, however, Bunyan is far from being an
advocate of women's liberation, particularly in the opening example of letting woman's helplessness be condemned from her own
mouth; for so speaks Mrs. Timorous: *"For if he, tho' a man, was
so hard put to it, what canst thou being but a poor Woman do?"*[20]
When the Reliever saves the women from their attackers, Bunyan
must make a general case for "we lose for want of asking." The
result is, "*...I marvelled much when you was entertained at the
Gate above, being ye knew that ye were but weak Women, that you
petitioned not the Lord there for a Conductor....*"[21] The same
view is shared by Great-heart, and the Interpreter recognizes sex
differences and treats the women accordingly: "I chose, my
Darlings, to lead you into the Room where such things are, because
you are Women, and they are easie for you."[22] The air of con-
descension is complicated by the reader's recollection that this form
of address is reserved in *The Holy War* for Diabolus' salutations to
his henchmen and victims. The impression is created that Bunyan
would please the ladies if he could, but that his first allegiance, as in
Part I, is to the *pilgrim,* of whatever sex, though males seem "more

equal" than others. As the Keeper of the Gate tells Mercy, "...I pray for all them that believe on me, by what means soever they come unto me."[23] This view represents what Roger Sharrock calls Bunyan's Open Communion ideal of reconciling minor theological differences in order to bring as many as possible to the pilgrim's road.[24]

At least one of the women in Part II receives bounteous treatment. Mercy is such a fully developed character that she almost threatens the security of the allegory. She gives rise to Christiana's "Bowels [compassion] becometh Pilgrims," a statement that is often taken as the motto of this continuation. She is a "poor Maid" who "falls in love with her own salvation" and swoons outside the Porter's Gate. She is courted by Brisk; and, as Rosemary Freeman points out,[25] her "I might a had Husbands afore now" can scarcely be taken allegorically. Her potential union with Brisk and the marriage of her sister, Bountiful, expand the warning of *Badman* against marrying with unbelievers and strangers and are reminiscent of the more serious treatment of this theme in Milton's *Samson Agonistes*. It can be speculated that, for all the richness of Mercy's story, she came to Bunyan first through Brisk himself. The term "brisk" is a popular seventeenth-century word used by Bunyan to castigate his own moral conversion in *Grace Abounding* — he is a "brisk talker," and Ignorance in Part I is a "brisk lad." Bunyan perhaps thought of Mercy in connection with the Christ-centered stages of conversion that oppose the "brisk" works of the man-centered moral stage.

Mercy and Christiana at one point become problematical characters rather in the manner of Ignorance of Part I. Neither is very charitable toward Simple, Sloth, and Presumption; but Mercy, because of her name, almost outrages the reader's sensibilities with her "...*let them hang and their Names Rot ... I think it a high favour that they were hanged afore we came hither, who knows else what they might a done to such poor Women as we are?*"[26] She then proceeds to turn this inflammatory rhetoric into a song, and there is again trouble reading this episode allegorically. Bunyan will accept no excuses for leaving Pilgrimage Road or for having a false conception of what it entails. The tone of Part II may be, overall, the community of believers; but the ferocity of Mercy and Christiana permits no softening of the spiritual fiber.

CHAPTER 7

Bunyan and the Emblem:
A Book for Boys and Girls *and*
The Pilgrim's Progress

I   A Book for Boys and Girls

A.   *History and Contents*

ALTHOUGH critics often present Bunyan as coming at the end of the tradition of allegory, he also came toward the end of another tradition that has much in common with allegory — the emblem. At first secular and then predominantly religious, emblems flourished in the sixteenth and seventeenth centuries. In Bunyan's period, they had become popular among Puritans largely through the influence of the collections of Francis Quarles and George Wither; but the audience for emblems was now mainly the lower classes. Bunyan was probably familiar with the works of Quarles and Wither; but his own emblem book, *A Book for Boys and Girls,* is, as Rosemary Freeman has indicated,[1] quite inventive. While it loosely fulfills the standard definition of emblems as symbolic pictures with explanatory mottos and poems, it combines forms, many of which are made emblematic only through Bunyan's application of them.

The history of Bunyan's emblem book is peculiar. At first entitled *A Book for Boys and Girls: Or, Country Rhymes for Children* (1686), with seventy-four pieces but *no illustrations,* it was revised in 1701 as *A Book for Boys and Girls or Temporal Things Spiritualised;* and twenty-five of the original emblems were omitted. In this form, it was exceedingly popular in the early eighteenth century, but later editions added woodcuts and had the title *Divine Emblems.* The original title's emphasis on children is somewhat misleading; for, of the sixteen verses composing Bunyan's prefatory "To the Reader," only the last two turn from "artificial babes" — "boys with beards, and girls that be / Big as old women, wanting gravity" — to real children. Adults, according to Bunyan, are children because they chase "the frantic fopperies of this age"; and, since ministers have failed with the thunderbolts of their sermons to force maturity on such spiritual children, he intends to educate these "dwarfs" in his own fashion. It is obvious that Bunyan's audience is *all* would-be believers; but he initially sets special snares for children with alphabets, spelling aids, figures, and a list of girls' and boys' names.

His preface is, in his usual vein, a good introduction to many of the themes of the emblems. He could, he maintains, use "higher strains" (the claim he made so decisively in the preface to *Grace Abounding*), but Scripture is again his key: Paul seemed to play the fool to win souls; Solomon sent fools to ants; and God spoke often through swallows, cuckoos, and the ass. "Great things, by little ones, are made to shine"; and, if Bunyan is pressed with the "inconsiderableness" of his objects, he has only to point out Samson's jawbone and Shamgar's oxgoad.

Perhaps because the poems were originally published without illustrations, or perhaps simply because of Bunyan's facility for vivid description, the first part of his emblem-poems usually provides a detailed word-picture of the subject and is then often followed by a section entitled "Comparison," which points the "moral." In such cases, the first part of the poem could easily function as a separate unit. Sometimes the pattern is altered, however, as in "Meditations Upon an Egg" (III), where one line of "narrative" is complemented by a line of "application": "The Egg's no chick by falling from the hen; / Nor man a Christian till he's born again." Occasionally, the whole is moral:

> Children become, while little, our delights,
> When they grow bigger, they begin to fright's.
> Their sinful nature prompts them to rebel,
> And to delight in paths that lead to Hell.
> Their parents' love and care they overlook,
> As if relation had them quite forsook.
> They take the counsels of the wanton's rather
> Than the most grave instructions of a father.
> They reckon parents ought to do for them
> Though they the fifth commandment do contemn.

> They snap and snarl, if parents them control,
> Though but in things most hurtful to the soul.[2]

This first verse of "Upon the Disobedient Child" (LXVI) might
have come directly from Attentive in *Badman*. It has the same lack
of sympathy for children and parents, and its brutal ending —
"They brought this bird up to pick out their eyes" — anticipates
the scare tactic of the eagle rhyme that Stephen Dedalus remembers
in the opening pages of James Joyce's *A Portrait of the Artist as a
Young Man*. Fortunately, this mode is infrequent in the Bunyan
collection.

There are also some paraphrases among Bunyan's emblem-
poems. The first poem is a ten-line delivery of the Ten Com-
mandments:

> Thou shalt not have another God but Me:
> Thou shalt not to an image bow the knee.
> Thou shalt not take the Name of God in vain:
> See that the sabbath thou do not profane.
> Honour thy father and thy mother too:
> In act, or thought, see thou no murder do.
> From fornication keep thy body clean:
> Thou shalt not steal, though thou be very mean.
> Bear no false witness; keep thee without spot;
> What is thy neighbour's, see thou covet not.

While the Lord's Prayer gains little in its revised form (IV), the
treatment of the Apostle's Creed (X) shows an interesting adaptive
technique; its second verse runs:

> Moreover I believe
> In God, the Holy Ghost;
> And that there is an Holy Church,
> An universal host.
> Also I do believe
> That sin shall be forgiven;
> And that the dead shall rise; and that
> The saints shall dwell in Heaven.

Bunyan's verses themselves, to be kind, are unpolished. Perhaps
an excessive example of their rhyming ability is "This Moses was a
fair and comely man; / His Wife a swarthy Ethiopian" ("Of

Moses and His Wife,'' XXXII). By contrast, there is evidence of some professionalism when Bunyan returns to a standard theme in "Upon the Barren Fig-Tree in God's Vineyard" (XXXIII) in which each of the six verses adapts to a common last line, "Bear fruit, or else thine end will cursed be!''; in "Upon the Fish in the Water" (VII) in which each of the three stanzas begins "The water is the Fish's element''; and in "Upon the Horse and His Rider" (XLI) in which the Comparison has a two-line refrain with variations.

Bunyan also displays his usual versatility with proverbs, for he adapts "beauty is only skin-deep" in "Of Beauty" (LXXIV), one of the few poems dealing with an abstraction and one which offers an interesting version of the *carpe diem* or "seize-the-day" topos:

> Beauty at best is but as fading flowers,
> Bright now, anon with darksome clouds it lowers;
> 'Tis but skin-deep, and therefor must decay;
> Time's blowing on it sends it quite away.
>
> Then why should it be, as it is, admired
> By one and t'other, and so much desired?
> Things flitting we should moderately use,
> Or we by them ourselves shall much abuse.

Much cleverer is the reversal of the proverb "Never let the right hand know what the left is doing" in "On the Cackling of a Hen" (LII) in which some "professors" of religion laud themselves as a hen cackles over an egg: "They can't but cackle on't where'er they go, / And what their right hand doth their left must know.''

Sheer realism abounds in some of the emblem-poems, and one can easily see that Bunyan would attract adults as well as attentive children and do so without the aid of pictures. The barren fig (XXXIII) is reprimanded sharply ("What, barren here!") as the expostulator creates a vivid picture of tree husbandry ("Hast not been digged about and dunged too?''). "Upon the Begger" (XXXIX) is quite effective in presenting from the third person a sight of the subject's being repulsed again and again by those to whom he sues for alms and of his finally winning because he will simply not be discouraged. Bunyan uses a definite crescendo of response and counterresponse, and the effect becomes somewhat humorous with the revelation of the Comparison that the beggar represents those who pray to God for mercy: "There's nothing like to importunity." To a lesser degree, Bunyan captures the postures of different riders, including the "tantivy" trot, in "Upon the Horse and His Rider" (XLI) and the details of watch care in "The Boy and Watch-maker" (XLVI).

Bunyan is also quite good at creating sound effects through words: the "slapping" sound as the fly attacks the candle in "Of the Fly at the Candle" (XXII); the "ting and tang," as well as the "ding, dong, bell," which he probably remembered from childhood jingles, of "Upon a Ring of Bells" (XXIX); and the "grunts" and "rustles" that disturb the subject's conscience in "Upon the Thief" (XXX), a poem that explains why "Old Tod" of *Badman* turned himself over to the authorities. The last line — "Few go to [eternal] life who do the gallows climb" — is a ringing conclusion to the psychology of the entire poem. But the tour de force, perhaps of the whole book, is "Of the Fatted Swine" (XXIV), in which the narrator is again an expostulator who delivers a verbal tirade about the hog/professor of religion who feels secure as a result of his "fattening up" by the world. The hog is invoked by "Sirrah!" and the whole is marvelously mock-heroic, as in "come, my gruntling," yet it is realistic as it passes from the hog's "snortings," "boarish looks" [a pun?], and "hoggish sportings" to its "shrill cries" when butchering time arrives. The language is as colloquial and "rough" in this poetic medium as it sometimes is in Bunyan's prose:

> Ah, Sirrah! I perceive thou art corn-fed,
> With best of hog's meat thou art pampered,
> Thou wallowest in thy fat; up thou art stalled;
> Art not, as heretofore, to hog's wash called.
> Thine orts lean pigs would leap at, might
>   they have it!
> One may see, by their whining, how they crave it.
>
> But Hog, why look'st so big? Why dost so flounce,
> So snort, and fling away? Dost now renounce
> Subjection to thy lord, 'cause he has fed thee?
> Thou art yet but a hog; of such he bred thee.
> Lay by thy snorting, do not look so big,
> *What was thy predecessor but a pig?*
>
> But come, my gruntling, when thou art full-fed,
> Forth to the butcher's stall thou must be led.
> Then will an end be put unto thy snortings,
> Unto thy boarish looks and hoggish sportings;

> Then thy shrill cries will echo in the air;
> Thus will my pig, for all his greatness, fare.

COMPARISON.

> This emblem shews some men are in this life
> Like full-fed hogs prepared for the knife.
> It likewise shews some can take no reproof
> More than the fatted hog, who stands aloof;
> Yea, that they never will for mercy cry
> Till time is past, and they for sin must die.

The subject matter alone of "Upon a Reeking Breath" (LV) and "Upon the Fly-Blows" (LX) is enough to demonstrate why some eighteenth-century editors made excisions. Bunyan can be very explicit: the reeking breath "comes from a foul stomach, or what's worse / Ulcerous lungs, teeth, or a private curse," a view that recalls the ravages of the disordered life of Badman. The humor of "Upon the Fly-Blows," again perhaps a kind of mock-heroism, results from the mixture of different levels of language: "Bloweth thereon, and so bemaggots it" versus "Now is not this a prejudicial fly?" Similarly, the child of God is not "one of whom men catch the scab, or itch" in "Upon the Chalk-Stone" (LIV). The fact that "Christ familiar speech doth use, / To make us to Him be recon-cil'd" in "Of the Child with the Bird at the Bush" (XXXI) does not entirely justify Bunyan's poetic diction, no matter how amusing it may be to his devotees.

B. *The Vanity of the World*

A number of the poems of *A Book for Boys and Girls* deal with the vanity of worldly things, a motif strong in biblical and in literary tradition and present in Bunyan's own Vanity Fair and Mrs. Bubble of *The Pilgrim's Progress*. The frog (XXXVI), the mole (XIX), and the boy with his plums (XLVII) and his hobbyhorse (LXVII) are used to make Bunyan's point; but the best illustration is the butterfly (XXI), which confirms that adults are being courted as an audience for these poems:

> Men seem in choice than children far more wise,
> Because they run not after Butterflies;

And yet, alas! for what are empty toys,
They follow children, like to beardless Boys.

Bunyan thought of the butterfly as a symbol of the world's fopperies; and he used it, along with another favorite, the spider, in *Christian Behaviour* (1663): "...thou wilt then see there is other things to mend than to imitate the butterfly. Alas, all these kind of things are but a painting the devil, and a setting a carnal gloss upon a castle of his; thou art but making gay the spider...."[3] "Of the Boy and Butterfly" is also notable for its description of the boy as he chases the creature and calls out to his friends:

He halloos, runs, and cries out, *Here, boys, here!*
Nor doth he brambles or the nettles fear;
He stumbles at the mole-hills, up he gets,
And runs again, as one bereft of wits....

Two other emblems, in this case "poems of manners," complete this theme. In "Upon Over-Much Niceness" (XII), people worry about their bodies and homes and are coy about their diet while they "their crying souls with hog's meat quiet." The four-line poem "Upon Apparel" (XVI) contrasts hiding one's nakedness with parading an unclean mind through excessive attention to clothing:

God gave us Clothes to hide our nakedness,
And we by them do it expose to view,
Our pride and unclean minds, to an excess,
By our apparel we to others shew.

Many of the emblems of *The Pilgrim's Progress* are on this same topos of the vanity of the world. The "grave person" (possibly meant to represent the poet Francis Quarles) with the world behind his back and the crown over his head has his opposite in the famous Muckraker,[4] who only looks downward and is unaware of the figure who holds the crown over his head. Passion represents "the men of this world," and his story is a kind of rewriting of the parable of the Prodigal Son and perhaps, along with that of Patience, of the Jesuit emblem figures of Amor and Anima. His counterpart, Patience, waits for the rewards of the next world and turns away from the material values for which Passion lusts. The man in the iron cage possesses eyes that can (must) gaze downward to where he has given his soul for the lusts, pleasures, and profits of this world. The man who dreams of Judgment has also lost salvation through his lust after worldly goods. Stand-fast, on the other hand, escapes because he rejects the world in the form of the infamous Madam Bubble, whose portrait was probably influenced by an emblem of Quarles. Behind all of these portraits, as behind Vanity Fair, is Ecclesiastes' "Vanity of vanities, saith the Preacher, vanity of vanities; all is vanity.... I have seen all the works that are done under the sun; and, behold, all is vanity and vexation of spirit" (1:2, 14).

C. *The Sun*

Several of the emblems of *A Book for Boys and Girls* console by associating the rising of the sun and the conditions of weather in general with God's mercy. "Meditations Upon the Peep of Day" (V) reminds the reader of Evangelist and Christian discussing the Wicket-gate, for its narrator cannot tell whether day has come: "I fancy that I see a little light, / But cannot yet distinguish day from night." The moral pointing of the final lines parallels Christian's belief in the light that Evangelist tries to show him: "Thus 'tis with such, who grace but now possessed; / They know not yet if they are curst or blessed." "On the Rising of the Sun" (XXV) is a more positive statement of the same theme, as its epithet "brave Sol" suggests; and "Meditations Upon Day Before the Sun-rising" (XVIII) makes a similar link between the Redeemer's grace and the sun. A more artful poem is "Upon the Sun's Reflection on the Clouds in a Fair Morning" (XV), which ingeniously relates the prayers of saints and "smoky curdled clouds":

> Look yonder! ah! methinks mine eyes do see
> Clouds edged with silver, as fine garments be!
> They look as if they saw that golden face,
> That makes black clouds most beautiful with grace.
>
> Unto the saints' sweet incense, or their prayer,
> These smoky curdled clouds I do compare.
> For as these clouds seem edged, or laced with gold,
> Their prayers return with blessings manifold.

A "lowering morning" (XI) bodes well instead of ill, for it is like the Gospel, thus inducing a sense of sin so that "we can weep till weeping does us good."

"Of the Going Down of the Sun" (XXXV) captures the emotions through which the anguished run as they watch the sun disappear. The Comparison says that the summer of the Gospel has passed unnoticed and asks whether our Sun — hopefully, the standard Renaissance pun on *Son,* though Bunyan retains "it" as the pronoun — will go down: "Let not the voice of night-birds us afflict, / And of our mis-spent summer us convict." In this group should also be included the four-line "Upon Time and Eternity" (LXXII), whose opening, *"Eternity* is like unto a ring," vaguely reminds one of Henry Vaughan's "The World."

D. *Music*

Two of the emblems, "Of the Rose-Bush" (XXXIV) and "Of the Child with the Bird at the Bush" (XXXI) were originally prefaced by music. And one would almost have to believe that Bunyan knew and used the tradition of merging poetry and music, part of the general Renaissance belief in the poetical nature of the arts (*ut poesis artes*) were it not for the influence of Revelation, which is acknowledged as his justification for musical metaphors in Part II of *The Pilgrim's Progress.* Nonetheless, "Upon a Skilful Player on an Instrument" (LIX) testifies to the same power of music that is expressed in John Dryden's "Alexander's Feast"; Bunyan writes:

> He that can play well on an instrument,
> Will take the ear and captivate the mind
> With mirth or sadness, for that it is bent
> Thereto as music, in it, place doth find!

The poem is a reworking of Bunyan's account of the tinkling cymbal, the skillful player, and the operation of grace in *Grace Abounding.* In the emblem, the musician is the minister of the Gospel as Bunyan effectively brings together the Puritan emphasis on preaching and on the aural sense. Conversely, the unskilled player (XL) is like the novice in "things divine"; he abuses rather than savors Scripture. In "Of the Child with the Bird at the Bush" (XXXI), the child (Christ) entices the bird (the sinner) with the "unthought-of music" of heaven, a phrase that is somewhat similar to the "inexpressive nuptial song" of Milton's "Lycidas."

Perhaps the most interesting of Bunyan's poems about music is "Upon a Ring of Bells," where the anatomized bells allegorize the human: the bells are the powers of the soul; the clappers, the passions; the steeple, the body. Bunyan has converted his youthful addiction to bell ringing into a request that God keep his "belfry key" and ward off others who would distract him from God. Like John Donne, the speaker would be made "God's music":

> O Lord! If Thy poor child might have his will,
> And might his meaning freely to Thee tell,
> He never of this music has his fill;
> There's nothing to him like Thy ding, dong, bell.

E. *Recurring Bunyan Themes and Motifs*

As has been suggested, many of the emblems in *A Book for Boys and Girls* reflect Bunyan's earlier works and interests. "The Sinner and the Spider" (XVII) and "The Boy and Watch-Maker" (XLVI) are dialogues, the form Bunyan had used in *Badman*. "Meditations Upon a Candle" (XIII) justifies his stance as the Chief of Sinners in *Grace Abounding:* "And biggest Candles give the better light, / As grace on biggest sinners shines most bright." It also promotes the sharing of spiritual adventures, the motif so prominent throughout *The Pilgrim's Progress,* in "The Candle shines to make another see; / A saint unto his neighbour light should be"; and it establishes the importance of the sense of hearing to the spiritual process: "And grace the heart first reaches through the ear." The "journey-to-heavenly-bliss" theme is reworked in "On the Postboy" (XXVII) and in "Upon the Horse and His Rider" (XLI), which also surveys different kinds of professors of religion.

The fear of conversion's coming too late, which obsesses Bunyan in *Grace Abounding* and plagues Christiana in *The Pilgrim's Progress,* Part II, is presented in "Of the Fatted Swine" (XXIV) and in "Upon the Thief" (XXX). "Of the Cuckoo" (XX) and "Upon the Frog" (XXXVI) offer comparisons with Formalist and Hypocrisy, respectively. The cuckoo is a "booby," as ineffectual in the world of man as is the spiritual adherent to the letter of the Law: "The formalist we may compare her to, / For he doth suck our eggs, and sing *Cuckoo!*" The four-line presentation of the frog, who "sits somewhat ascending," is followed by an eight-line Comparison that drives toward the definition of the hypocrite: "And

though he seeks in churches for to croak / He neither loveth Jesus,
nor His yoke." Christian charges both Formalist and Hypocrisy
with "walking by the rude working of [their] fancies" rather than
"by the Rule of my Master."

Different aspects of the Law and the Gospel, with special value
for Bunyan's pictures of legalistic professors, of the carnal stage of
conversion, and of Adam the first and Moses are touched on in
"Upon the Whipping of a Top" (XXXVII), where the top is the
legalist; in "Of the Rose-bush" (XXXIV), where the bush stands
for Adam's race and the rose for Christ; and in "Of Moses and His
Wife" (XXXII), "Upon Death" (LVI), and "Upon a Pair of Spec-
tacles" (LXIII). "Upon a Reeking Breath" (LV) is reminiscent of
Bunyan's description of the Ranters and the Quakers in *Grace
Abounding* who imbibe Scripture but corrupt it, and the corrupters
of "good doctrine" are reviled in "Upon the Fly-blows" (LX) as
once again Bunyan associates *maul* with the diabolical: "Reproach
it then, thou art a mauling club, / This fly; yea, and the son of
Beelzebub."

The image of the fowler, which Bunyan used to justify his own
artistic methods in the preface to *The Pilgrim's Progress,* Part I,
but which, with his nets and snares, usually connotes evil, becomes
an emblem for the Devil in "Upon the Lark and the Fowler"
(XXIII) and in "Upon Our Being Afraid of the Apparition of Evil
Spirits" (LXV). Mercy's longing for the mirror, an ambiguous
symbol at best, is supported by "Upon a Looking-Glass"
(XLVIII), for it becomes the Word of God in which blind men "so
often read / Their judgment . . . and do it nothing dread."

"Of the Horse and Drum" (LI) introduces various kinds of
"professors" of religion again, but the horses who are frightened
by the drum evoke Diabolus' psychological use of this instrument
in *The Holy War.* Matthew and the green plums are called up by
"Of Physic" (LXII) and "Upon the Boy and His Paper of Plums"
(LXVII). "Of Moses and His Wife" (XXXII) recalls Geoffrey Whitney's emblem on the Ethiopian, as well as Fool and Want-wit trying
to wash the Ethiopian white, the emblem that the shepherds show
to Christiana and her companions. The very spirit of Part II of *The
Pilgrim's Progress,* with its great variety of flowers in the garden of
Beulah, breathes in "Of Fowls Flying in the Air" (XLIII), which
enumerates the different qualities of professors who will get to
heaven and the various nations they will represent:

Methinks I see a sight most excellent,
All sorts of birds fly in the firmament,
Some great, some small, all of a diverse kind,
Mine eye affecting, pleasant to my mind.
Look how they tumble in the wholesome air,
Above the world of worldlings, and their care!

And as they diverse are in bulk and hue,
So are they in their way of flying too.

So many birds, so many various things,
Tumbling in th' element upon their wings.

The last two lines of this first part of the poem are among Bunyan's most felicitous artistically, and the "doctrine" of its Comparison contrasts with the dangers outlined for marriage with unbelievers in *Badman* and in *The Pilgrim's Progress,* Part II. The whole section is, in fact, a beautiful expression of Bunyan's contention that the ways to God are many and that judgment of them should be guarded and tolerant.

The long poem, "The Awakened Child's Lamentation" (II), deserves attention not only for its psychological insight and authentic notes of the child's voice but also for the remarkable fact that, as E. S. Buchanan has said of "Meditations upon a Candle,"[5] it is a "poetic compendium of *Grace Abounding*" — but on a child's level. Though the child's "filth boils" in this poem and though it feels "benighted," the spiritual horrors are far less frightful than in other contemporary Puritan literature for children.[6] Bunyan seldom becomes more terrifying than in the opening line of "Upon Death" (LVI): "Death's a cold comforter to girls and boys."

In *A Confession of My Faith* (1672), Bunyan had declared his esteem for water baptism and for the sacrament of the Lord's Supper, but he had not found them fundamental to church membership. In "Upon the Sacraments" (XIV), their relationship to ransom is disavowed: "Bread, wine, nor water, me no ransom bought." As might also be expected, many of the other emblem-poems demonstrate the importance Bunyan attached to Christ, but his poem "Of the Love of Christ" (L) comes closest to his feeling in the latter part of *Grace Abounding;* man cannot comprehend the "large dimensions" of the love of Christ should he "dilate thereon world without end." "Of the Spouse of Christ" (LVIII) is interesting for its use of Canticles and Revelation, which were untiring sources for Bunyan's imagery. This poem is marred, however, by

124 JOHN BUNYAN

the moral of the last verse, a warning against pride that has little to
do with the beautiful relationship hitherto depicted:

> Take heed of pride, remember what thou art
> By nature, though thou hast in grace a share;
> Thou in thyself dost yet retain a part
> Of thine own filthiness: wherefore beware.

F. *The Barren-Tree Motif*

The interest in profit motives of *Badman* is revived in a number
of poems on the barren tree, but the fruit that must be harvested is
the soul. Bunyan treats this theme, an habitual subject with Puritan
writers,[7] at length in *The Barren Fig-tree; Or, The Doom and
Downfall of the Fruitless Professor* (ca. 1673). In this prose work,
he sounds what becomes a preferred term, "cumber-ground" professor, an adaptation of the language of the Authorized Version of
the Bible; and he uses it to address the barren fig tree in Emblem
XXXIII: "O cumber-ground, thou art a barren tree; / Bear fruit,
or else thine end will cursed be!" The apple tree is treated similarly
in "Upon the Promising Fruitfulness of a Tree" (XXVI), which is a
rewriting also of the Parable of the Sower and a parallel for Eve's
apple in the Palace Beautiful and for the discussion of the dish of
apples at Gaius' inn. In "Upon the Vine-Tree" (XLV), a fruitless
vine is not worth a "fly," and fruitless professors are not worth a
"pin." The same demand to produce spiritually or be damned lies
behind the emblems of the field of straw and the tree that is rotten
on the inside in *The Pilgrim's Progress,* Part II.

G. *The Creatures*

Bunyan's interest in the creatures derives from the tradition of
the "book of nature," which he calls the "book of creatures" in
The Resurrection of the Dead (1665),[8] and from the biblical tradition of "Go to the ant thou sluggard." He uses this injunction in
the preface to and in Emblem XXXVIII, "Upon the Ant," of *A
Book for Boys and Girls;* and he awakens Christian with it in Part I
of *The Pilgrim's Progress*. Bunyan may also have been influenced
by the small creatures that fascinated classical writers and that continued to appear in the works of Robert Herrick and others in the
seventeenth century. Some of Bunyan's creature emblems are oddi-

ties. He entitles LXIV, for example, "Upon Our Being Afraid of Small Creatures," a view that runs counter to traditional treatments. "Upon the Bee" (IX) links that insect with sin — unusual in light of Renaissance concern for the efficiency of the hive and its political overtones and of Bunyan's own "nu honey from a *B*" in *The Holy War*. One of his best poems, LVII, rebaptizes the traditional snail as an emblem of the professor who goes softly but surely to heaven:

> She goes but softly, but she goeth sure,
> She stumbles not, as stronger creatures do.
> Her journey's shorter, so she may endure
> Better than they which do much further go.
>
> She makes no noise, but stilly seizeth on
> The flower or herb appointed for her food;
> The which she quietly doth feed upon,
> While others range, and glare, but find no good.
>
> And though she doth but very softly go,
> However 'tis not fast, nor slow, but sure;
> And certainly they that do travel so,
> The prize they do aim at they do procure.
>
> COMPARISON.
>
> Although they seem not much to stir, less go,
> For Christ that hunger, or from wrath that flee,
> Yet what they seek for quickly they come to,
> Though it doth seem the farthest off to be.
>
> One act of faith doth bring them to that Flower,
> They so long for, that they may eat and live;
> Which to attain is not in others' power,
> Though for it a king's ransom they would give.
>
> Then let none faint, nor be at all dismayed,
> That life by Christ do seek, they shall not fail
> To have it; let them nothing be afraid;
> The herb and flower are eaten by the Snail.

As a result of these emblems, one cannot agree with F. J. Harvey Darton that Bunyan almost tortured his mind to find his morals.[9] The finest of the emblems of the creatures — and the longest and the finest of the lot — is "The Sinner and the Spider" (XVII). The sinner salutes the spider as a black, "ugly crawling thing" and opens himself to its "lecture." Man may be made in God's image, the spider rejoinders, but man has betrayed God and himself. The spider is still in the primitive condition in which God made it, except, of course, for what it has lost through man's ambition. Bunyan produces a strongly developed sense of the suffering of the creatures through man's fall and of the test of worth as right usage.

The spider's venom is good because God made it, an argument that recalls Gaius' poem on apples in *The Pilgrim's Progress,* Part II. Man is a self-murderer, but the spider willingly hurts no one. The sinner blusters about the natural antipathy between men and spiders and threatens to crush his talkative opponent. The spider is oblivious: "Yet I will speak, I can but be rejected: / Sometimes great things by small means are effected." It spins and weaves, the spider admits, to let men see that their best performances are but cobwebs, a view that echoes Bunyan's old theme of the profitlessness of good works alone. The sinner, educated in the "mysteries" of the web, vows that he will be no more a derider. But the spider is as determined to win this man as the Interpreter is to conquer Christian, and the sinner is "caught" when a four-fold way to hell is laid open by spider rhetoric: "O Spider, thou delight'st me with thy skill; / I pr'ythee, spit this venom at me still." The spider's description of getting into the palace adapts Proverbs 30:28 ("The spider taketh hold with her hands, and is in king's palaces") and becomes a miniature allegory of the journey to God; and Christ is identified as the door, just as he was as the Wicket-gate in *The Pilgrim's Progress.* The poem finally ends with the sinner's admission that he has been a fool — "They learn may, that to Spiders go to school."

This insect had always fascinated Bunyan, and one of the most famous emblems of the Interpreter's House in *The Pilgrim's Progress* is the spider on the wall of the beautiful room. Christiana and Mercy find themselves confronted with a riddle, as well as an emblem, and blush when they are forced to admit that there are more spiders in the room than they had thought.[10] In this instance, the spider shows that man (or woman) may be more venomous than the most venomous of creatures; and the insect's "laying hold with its hands in kings' palaces" motivates Christians to "lay hold" by the hand of faith. Part I contains a subtle reemphasis of the overt handling of a similar theme when, after the first emblem, the Interpreter sets a pattern of taking Christian by the hand to lead him to the next scene. As U. Milo Kaufman points out,[11] the hand was frequently associated with faith in Puritan literature. The effect is to interlock the adventures of both sets of travelers in the Interpreter's House.

Much more conventionally, the spider appears as a symbol of sin in the emblem of the robin and the spider of Part II. Two poems of *A Book for Boys and Girls,* "Of Man By Nature" (LXI) and "Meditations Upon an Egg" (III), draw the same conclusions as Christiana and Mercy: man can have more venom than the spider. This same belief appears twice in Bunyan's *A Discourse of the . . . Houses of God* (1688) and once in *The Resurrection of the Dead* (1665). The spider symbolizes lost souls in *Light for Them that Sit in Darkness* (1675): "The fly in the spider's web is an emblem of the soul in such a condition — the fly is entangled in the web; at this the spider shows himself; if the fly stir again, down comes the spider to her, and claps a foot upon her; if yet the fly makes a noise, then with poisoned mouth the spider lays hold upon her; if the fly struggle still, then he poisons her more and more. What shall the fly do now? Why, she dies, if somebody does not quickly release her."[12] For Bunyan, the "release" is Christ.

H.   *Emblems of Everyday Life*

Many of the emblems involving homely objects and contemporary sights seem, by subject at least, more derivative: the lantern for grace (XLIX), the chalk-stone for the child of God (LIV), the hourglass for man's life (LIII), fire for hell (LXXIII), and a weathercock for the Christian braving Antichrist (LXIX). On the other hand, "Upon a Penny Loaf" (XLIV) relates inflation to the worth of God's Word during famines of the soul: "Thy price one penny is, in time of plenty; / In famine, doubled 'tis from one to twenty." When men fear death, God's Word becomes "[their] all, [their] life, [their] breath." Although the candle has often been an emblem, Bunyan is quite original when he develops a domestic incident in "Upon the Sight of a Pound of Candles Falling to the Ground" (XLII). The one candle left standing is Christ; and the fallen candles are the "bulk of God's elect, in their lapsed state." The first part of the poem mimics the voices of those confronted with this household crisis:

> But be the candles down, and scatter'd too?
> Some lying here, some there? What shall we do?

> Hold, light the candle there that stands on high,
> It you may find the other candles by.
> Light that, I say, and so take up the pound
> You did let fall, and scatter on the ground.

II   *Bunyan and the Emblem Tradition*

The habit of thought demonstrated by *A Book for Boys and Girls* is probably as much the result of the use of similitude in the Puritan tradition as of the genre of the emblem proper. Bunyan avows his allegiance to this kind of thought openly on the title pages of Parts I and II of *The Pilgrim's Progress*. Indeed, the whole tradition of typology, in which the Protestants had been influenced by the Catholics, in turn influenced the emblem, which was well developed by the Catholics themselves. In *Light for Them that Sit in Darkness* (1675), Bunyan cites Samson as a type of Christ and lists other types (the paschal lamb, the red cow, mannah, the rock, and Mount Moriah)[13] that easily suggest emblems. He speaks of many of these same objects under the term "riddles" at the feast of Emmanuel in *The Holy War;* and in *Badman,* he refers to the Lord's Day as an "emblem of the Sabbath."[14] He is so fond of certain episodes from the Bible — Joseph and Potiphar's wife, Esau's selling of his birthright, and Lot's wife — that he makes them emblems in their own right. Again, in *The Pilgrim's Progress,* Part I, and in *The Holy War,* the "engines" of biblical heroes become emblems after the fashion of the biblical metaphor, "the breastplate of righteousness." Thinking in emblematic terms was simply a habit with Bunyan, but he is no more specific in his use of the term *emblem* than in his use of *allegory.* In fact, the two are nearly synonymous terms in his mind and vary only according to length.

Where Bunyan acquired his notions of emblem cannot be finally resolved. He undoubtedly knew at least the works of Francis Quarles and George Wither, but he thought in emblematic terms throughout his career. In *Paul's Departure and Crown* (first printed in 1692), the apostle is likened to a nightingale with its breast upon a thorn;[15] Bunyan probably drew this "emblem" from legends of the bird's efforts to remain alert during its night vigil. But, among his sparse references to seventeenth-century literary figures is an allusion to a poet who was very much in the emblem tradition:

If what the learned Herbert says, holds true,
A verse may find him, who a sermon flies,
And turn delight into a sacrifice....[16]

III   *Emblem Method in* The Pilgrim's Progress, *Part I*

The outstanding quality of what Bunyan calls his "emblems" is his diversity in method of presentation, in both *A Book for Boys and Girls* and *The Pilgrim's Progress,* where the emblem is not of primary concern as such. Except for the picture of the "grave Person" (the ideal pastor), the emblems that Christian sees at the Interpreter's House in Part I are scenic, with persons moving before him. They are miniature dramas[17] that generally present examples of action and false action, but often both appear in the same frame. For example, the man who dusts without sprinkling is followed by the damsel who sprinkles and then sweeps; his false action is corrected by her right action. Patience not only is meaningful within her own emblem to offset the *im*patience of Passion, but she demonstrates what Christian lacks before this first bout with the emblems is over and he is pushing to be on the road. What is being thrown into relief is various kinds of action with patience a form of right "action" that is opposed not only to the self-assertion of so many of the characters throughout *The Pilgrim's Progress* but also to lassitude and despair as set forth by the man in the iron cage and by the experiences with the Giant Despair. The true greatness, then, of this "emblem theater"[18] is that the scenes are individually meaningful, while the effect of the whole is to salute right action; to warn Christian, the audience, and all wayfaring/warfaring Christians to be always watchful;[19] to proclaim watchfulness itself a kind of action; and to establish that, just as there are many kinds of "action," so there are many kinds of spiritual candidates.

The emblem that is most in accord with Christian's particular approach to the road is the man who fights his way through to the palace, but Christian must learn the efficaciousness of all of the emblems. Quite remarkable in this light is the variation in drawing what is labeled the "Comparison" in *A Book for Boys and Girls.* Although the Interpreter himself "interprets" most of the emblems, Christian actually participates, through the act of interpretation, in the emblems of the man in the iron cage and of the dreamer of Judgment as he discusses with them their own impressions of their experiences. He is thus being equipped for the cage into which he and Faithful are put at Vanity Fair and for the despair of Doubting Castle. In keeping with the purview of action, as well as with the desire for variety in presentation, Bunyan has Christian at the Palace Beautiful pass from theater to museum as he inspects the records and relics of heroes of action and of faith and leaves "armed" for the battle against evil and temptation.

IV   *Emblem Method in* The Pilgrim's Progress, *Part II*

Christiana and her group see the emblems of Christian; but the additions, tailored to their specific needs, seem more derivative, although the style of presentation is original. Matthew's questions to Prudence in fact suggest that he has seen emblem books with conduits, a pelican, fire, candles, and a crowing cock, some of which are used as subjects in *A Book for Boys and Girls*. The "meditations for the way,"[20] such as the apples of Eve, the golden anchor, and Jacob's ladder, also seem quite standard to the tradition of the emblem. Again, however, Bunyan makes them his own by varying their form of presentation from museum piece to, at least with the anchor that Christiana receives, admission ticket and map of conduct for the way. Earlier Bunyan reversed the usual order — from indoctrination to practice of the principles set forth in the emblem — by having the action of the boys, who are out in front of the others until the lions threaten, become an emblem of boldness until danger looms. In this case, the subject matter is ordinary, but the route of usefulness has changed. Christiana's sons must rethink past experience; but the emblem they produce for others will, rightly used, dictate future action.

Similarly, Bunyan has the emblem scene of Mount Charity (the man with the bundle of cloth from which he constantly cuts garments for the poor without diminishing the bundle) become a justification after the fact for Mercy's services to the needy, which lost her the favor of Brisk. The very use of the mountains in the shepherds' scenes, of both Parts I and II, for delivering emblems and, through their names, for giving the morals of the emblems is a novelty in Bunyan's emblem techniques, though he has applied this device in the poem that Offor calls *Ebal and Gerizim*. In *The Pilgrim's Progress,* Part I, Mount Caution's blind men among the tombs are an explanation, with variations, for Christian and Hopeful's experience with Despair; and these men also vary the emblem style of Bunyan by having been derived directly from Scriptural metaphor: "The man that wandereth out of the way of understanding shall remain in the congregation of the dead" (Proverbs 21:16).

One of the best examples of the emblems of Part II that force the pilgrims and the audience to look back to Part I is Mercy's mirror. Immediately, one recalls Christian's attempt to look through the "perspective glass," that is, "through a glass darkly." Mercy's mirror, like that of the mirror emblem in *A Book for Boys and Girls,* is the Word of God; and she can see in its reflection not only herself but Christ. Except for the fact that "mercy" and mirrors are associated elsewhere in Bunyan, one might conclude that the author is lauding Mercy's spiritual situation over that of Christian.

The best gloss is the mirror emblem in Bunyan's *The Saint's Priviledge and Profit* (first printed in 1692), which is, as George Offor has noted, almost more of a riddle than an emblem. Bunyan might easily have introduced it by asking why the brazen laver, or basin, is made of women's looking glasses: "I read that the laver of brass and the foot of it was made of the looking-glasses of the women that assembled at the door of the tabernacle, Ex. xxxviii.8, methinks to signify, that men might see their smyrches when they came to wash; so here you see the law is placed even with the mercy-seat, only that stood above, whereby those that come to the throne of grace for mercy might also yet more be put in mind that they are sinners."[21] The link between Christ and mercy/Mercy is forged in the midst of Bunyan's all-important contrast between legalism and spirituality. Man's deformity is not denied in this selection from Bunyan's prose or in the Mercy episode, but these examples show to advantage beside the solemn and prejudging notes of Emblem XLVIII, "Upon a Looking-Glass." Whatever felicities are to be found in *A Book for Boys and Girls,* this work does not, as in the case of the mirror, consistently rise to Bunyan's full heights.

CHAPTER 8

Bunyan's Reputation and Importance

I *Reputation*

JOHN Bunyan knew the mixed blessing of achieving fame and notoriety during his own lifetime. By the last ten years of his life, he had ceased to be known only among his fellow Baptists and other sects with whom he had engaged in theological controversies and had become a great public figure. The Established Church and Charles II had been forced to recognize him, and James II sought his help. One of his publishers came to be called Nathaniel "Bunyan" Ponder through being associated with him. Many of his works were immensely popular; and *The Pilgrim's Progress,* Part I, went through eleven editions while he was living.

The tinker's friend, Charles Doe, a Southwark comb-maker, secured from his widow ten unpublished manuscripts, which Bunyan had prepared for the press, and published a folio edition of these and ten previously published pieces in 1692, the first volume of a collected edition that was not completed. The last section of this volume, which Doe called *The Struggler* (a reference to his own "struggles" with publication), contained an invaluable chronological catalog of all of Bunyan's works and a short biography of Bunyan. This work, along with several other late seventeenth-century biographies, gave the preacher a saintlike status. Among the most important of these narratives are the anonymous *An Account of the Life and Actions of John Bunyan* bound with the spurious *Third Part of The Pilgrim's Progress* in 1692; *A Continuation of Mr. Bunyan's Life* included in the seventh edition of *Grace Abounding* (also in 1692), perhaps by George Cokayne; and *An Account of the Life and Death of John Bunyan,* published in 1700 in the second edition of *The Heavenly Foot-man,* by someone who had known Bunyan in prison.

Bunyan was not always cherished by "polite readers," however;

and, until the end of the first quarter of the nineteenth century, he was generally considered a religious writer who fell outside the province of the men of letters. In fact, the eighteenth century was often contemptuous of his humble origin and trade. The Blue Stocking, Mrs. Elizabeth Montague, for example, dismissed Bunyan and Francis Quarles as "artificers in leather." On the other hand, the disparagement of Bunyan attributed to Joseph Addison — any author could gain admirers since Bunyan and Quarles pleased as many readers as John Dryden and John Tillotson — may not be by Addison after all. In addition, the reluctance of William Cowper in "Tirocinium" to name Bunyan, whom he admired but who was too "mean" to be considered fit company for polite audiences, has been muted by J. W. Mackail's suggestion that Cowper refers not to the low esteem of Bunyan but to the ludicrousness of his name, as was also the case with Thomas "Sprat" and Thomas "Flatman."[1] Although Bunyan was not perceived as a genuine literary figure, he was the object of random comments by some who *had* acquired such status in the eighteenth century: Samuel Richardson, Jonathan Swift,[2] and Samuel Johnson. In fact, Dr. Johnson abruptly removed Bishop Thomas Percy's little daughter from his knee and said that he would not give a farthing for her when she admitted that she had not read *The Pilgrim's Progress!*

The nineteenth century established Bunyan's literary reputation and influenced his modern assessment. Robert Southey's biography accompanied his 1830 edition of *The Pilgrim's Progress* for a more scholarly audience. Southey's high opinions of Bunyan were shared by Samuel Taylor Coleridge, who thought that *The Pilgrim's Progress* was the finest *Summa Theologicae Evangelicae* ever produced, and by Thomas Babington Macaulay, who reviewed the Southey edition in 1831 and wrote an article on Bunyan for the *Encyclopaedia Britannica.* Two trends developed in this period that affected Bunyan's reputation. During the 1840s, when the Evangelical movement was at its height, Bunyan again emerged as an outstanding religious figure. The editor of the standard edition of his works, George Offor, shows this Evangelical bias in his commentaries. On the other hand, the Romantics praised Bunyan as an unnurtured genius. They also interested themselves in his facility for weaving myths, a focus influenced, no doubt, by the famous "sleeping portrait" of Bunyan as the dreamer of *The Pilgrim's Progress,* which was prefixed to the third edition of 1679 and done by Robert White from his earlier pencil sketch.[3] Moreover, such preoccupations of the Romantics caused the critics of Bunyan to emphasize his artistic creativeness and to ignore his milieu. Finding the balance between these two areas has been the task of modern critics. An outstanding influence in establishing the relationship between Bunyan and his milieu is William York Tindall's *John Bunyan: Mechanick Preacher.*

II *Importance*

John Bunyan was and is a man of the people, and it will be interesting to see whether the current attractiveness of the "grass roots" will bring a popular revival of his works. As yet, only *Grace Abounding, The Pilgrim's Progress, The Life and Death of Mr. Badman,* and *The Holy War* are widely known outside scholarly circles. Students, who usually read only *The Pilgrim's Progress* and a selection from the spiritual autobiography, and who are mostly unfamiliar with his times, or at least with his theology, find him whimsical, free from affectation, and genial — and they love him accordingly. The present generation that chants, after J. R. R. Tolkien, "Frodo lives!" may well take Bunyan to its heart, as have past generations who grew up with the *Iliad* and the *Odyssey.*[4] And Bunyan, reflecting on his own early interest in such figures of romance as Bevis of Southampton and Guy of Warwick, might well not detest such chain-links of taste. He surely would not mind that students are better able to appreciate Revelation or Daniel or the Song of Songs because of his use of these sections of the Bible in *The Pilgrim's Progress,* a use that makes them suddenly become more comprehensible. While scholar-teachers try to prevent his major works from being entirely detached from their milieu, students want to read them, as they want to read the works of Milton, only as *literature.* But they do, for whatever reasons, continue to read them; and they may often agree with Huckleberry Finn's view that *The Pilgrim's Progress* is "about a man that left his family, it didn't say why" and that "The statements was interesting, but tough."[5]

No one is going to claim that John Bunyan ranks fourth after Shakespeare, Milton, and Chaucer in world literature or to believe with Macaulay that, with the exception of *The Pilgrim's Progress, The Holy War* is the best allegory ever written. Yet Bunyan does rank somewhere among the foremost authors. *The Pilgrim's Prog-*

ress itself is the culmination of one of the greatest literary traditions, allegory, which virtually disappeared as a formal genre after
Bunyan.[6] Bunyan is also the last of another great but lesser-known
tradition, the emblem, which is itself an adjunct of allegory. He
may well have fostered the development of the novel; and, with
other "Puritans," he surely influenced the trend of Restoration
prose toward the "plain style." He is the end product of the homi-
letic tradition that started in the Middle Ages; and he will continue
to be studied for his contributions to biography, autobiography,
prison literature, and various Puritan literary genres.

Bunyan caught the imaginations of such divergent and great figures as Benjamin Franklin; William Blake, who produced twenty-
nine watercolor paintings of *The Pilgrim's Progress;* Nathaniel
Hawthorne;[7] George Bernard Shaw; and e. e. cummings. William
Makepeace Thackeray's famous novel, *Vanity Fair,* owes its title to
Bunyan and Ecclesiastes. *The Holy War* was instrumental in the
writing of Benjamin Keach's *Progress of Sin* (1684) and may have
produced Hawthorne's portrait of John Endicott, especially if it
were read in the beautifully illustrated edition of George Burder.[8]
Its finest tribute, even so, is Rudyard Kipling's seven-stanza poem
by the same name — a poem that sees Bunyan as the prophet of
English events in 1917 and one that was singled out by T. S. Eliot
for a selected edition of Kipling's poetry. No work is more responsive to the man, Bunyan, and to his whole canon, however, than
Robert Browning's poem "Ned Bratts," "Written from memory of
Bunyan's story of old Tod in *The Life and Death of Mr. Badman.*"

Benjamin Disraeli called Bunyan "the Spenser of the people,"
while Thomas Adams chose to designate him "the Shakespeare of
the Puritans." Theodore Roosevelt was drawing on *The Pilgrim's
Progress* when he named the Muckraker Movement of the early
twentieth century. Music, through Vaughan Williams and through
opera, has claimed Bunyan, as has the ballet. His mastery of the
English language occupied the attentions of one class for an entire
term.[9] Bronson Alcott and Mahatma Gandhi both used *The Pilgrim's Progress* as a text book, and Louisa May Alcott had her
family in *Little Women* take it as a model for life. Richard Winboult Harding reports also that scenes from *The Pilgrim's Progress*
were frequently acted out by people undergoing treatment in the
Leper Settlement at Purulia, Behar, India.[10] A. C. Benson's novel,
Beside Still Waters, has the character Hugh Neville read *The Pilgrim's Progress* and ponder why critics have been less favorable to

Part II. George Bernard Shaw praised *Badman* as an economic document and had the last words of Valiant-for-truth read at his funeral, and Sir Winston Churchill is also reported to have had a portion of *The Pilgrim's Progress* used in his funeral services. The Welsh have even gone so far in idolizing Bunyan as to be willing to subscribe to editions of his lesser known theological works.[11]

As has been suggested, Bunyan has been enormously influential in America,[12] where *The Pilgrim's Progress* was one of the earliest books to be illustrated[13] and where Bunyan's vision helped to shape the symbolism of the American frontier and wilderness.[14] *The Pilgrim's Progress* appears on the all-time best-seller list in America, with *Grace Abounding* a near best-seller.[15]

Aldous Huxley may or may not be correct that "Parodies and caricatures are the most penetrating of criticisms," but most agree that they are a form of tribute. At least, one must have stature in order to be treated in this way. *The Pilgrim's Progress* is parodied in cummings' *The Enormous Room* to satirize, among other things, repression, conformity, and fastidiousness.[16] Parody is operative in Ronald A. Knox's article, "The Identity of the Pseudo-Bunyan,"[17] but the critics of Bunyan rather than the writer himself receive the brunt of the satire here. Knox attacks those who find it impossible to believe that a tinker could have written *The Pilgrim's Progress* and who use such methods as counting *you's* and *thou's* and translating "Sagacity" into "Saga-City" to make their cases. The parody resides mainly in the "names" of these critics: Canon Wrest-the-Word, Mr. Muck-rake, Canon Obvious, Mr. Jettison Cargo, Dr. Cheese-Paring, Mr. Book-worm, Bishop While-on-the-one-Hand. Finally, what should be the most famous parody of Bunyan's style is James Joyce's in the "Oxen of the Sun" episode of *Ulysses*. It is heavy-handed, and its circumlocution is not Bunyan's; but it has caught Bunyan's Puritan stress on the aural sense: "Heard he [Boasthard] then in that clap the voice of the god Bringforth or, what Calmer said, a hubbub of Phenomenon? Heard? Why, he could not but hear unless he had plugged up the tube Understanding (which he had not done). For through that tube he saw that he was in the land of Phenomenon where he must for a certain one day die...."[18]

In the end, John Bunyan stands as one of the greatest preachers and one of the kindliest purveyors of Calvinism that the Christian world has known. He not only paints the picture of the Puritan as the Puritan sees himself in *Grace Abounding,* but he is absolutely essential in getting past the generalizations about and the stereotypes of Puritanism. Bunyan of course lacks the full Renaissance humanism of Milton, but he complements it with his homeliness and his warmth, which are displayed so often in his love of music and in his demonstrations of the common touch. His humor, which is perhaps unexpected, particularly his propensity for punning, has not been given the attention it deserves. Too often, he is merely dismissed as a "hellfire-and-brimstone" preacher.

His sense of character seems instinctive, and he is uncanny in catching the speaking accents of figures who may be types but who are, simultaneously, uniquely themselves. If he often misquotes the King James or the Geneva Bibles, he also makes biblical characters and settings as lively and as integral to his works as is the English countryside — his own Midlands area in particular. Bunyan's Bible moves and breathes.

For the scholar, John Bunyan offers both literature and a firsthand look at seventeenth-century England and at the numbers of inspired "mechanicks" it produced. For the literary anthropologist and the historian, Bunyan is the type who was produced by a very special milieu; and he represents not merely his own class alone. His works contain, in domesticated form and fashion, many of the types, themes, and motifs of the Middle Ages and Renaissance. For the psychologist, he must seem to reconstitute faith in the racial unconscious and in the natural genius. For the psychoanalyst, he will be forever a classic case of the identity crisis. Bunyan is the kind of man about whom biographies for an audience of adolescents are written. He also endured the soul-crisis, the "dark night of the soul," that seems to be one of the hallmarks of the world's outstanding figures. And he provides a clue to the "some secret thing" at the heart of the artistic process. He deserves to be cherished for having made his imagination work for him in a time when imagination was still suspect.

Yet there is no need of patterning or propagandizing Bunyan's life toward encomiums of diligence and duty. He was what he was. His refusal to bend before his judges may have been frustrating to them, it may be simplistic to moderns, but it is the epitome of practicing what one preaches. The difficult part to believe is not that his death can be traced to another attempt to perform a good service, but that he should ever have been considered the "Chief of Sinners" — by himself or by anyone else.

All of this lavish praise would probably have been a surprise to

Bunyan; for, to him, there were essentially two kinds of people: the elect and the reprobate. Fortunately, he was caught up by the myriad of forms in each category. His Chaucerian joy in the diversity of human beings is nowhere better expressed than in the emblem-poem that has already been quoted but that merits repeating as an expression of Bunyan's views:

> Methinks I see a sight most excellent,
> All sorts of birds fly in the firmament.
> Some great, some small, all of a diverse kind,
> Mine eye affecting, pleasant to my mind.
> Look how they tumble in the wholesome air,
> Above the world of worldlings, and their care!
>
> And as they diverse are in bulk and hue,
> So are they in their way of flying too.
>
> So many birds, so many various things,
> Tumbling in th' element upon their wings.

Though he refers here to those who *will* get to heaven, the tone is responsive to the variety of humanity that he loved to make talk and move. The result is that, of his major works, only *Grace Abounding* is painful — though beautiful in its own way. *The Pilgrim's Progress, The Life and Death of Mr. Badman, The Holy War,* and *A Book for Boys and Girls* are, among many, many other things, good reading. They impress one with the feeling that, after John Bunyan was able to turn outward from himself, he was, for his times, an incredibly liberal man not only about methods of baptism, church membership, and routes to heaven but also about human differences.

Notes and References

Preface

1. Robert Conquest, "Christian Symbolism in *Lucky Jim*," *Critical Quarterly*, 7 (1965), 88, n. 2.
2. For the dates of publication of Bunyan's works, this study relies principally on Frank Mott Harrison, *A Bibliography of the Works of John Bunyan* (Oxford, 1932). For the dates of Bunyan's life, it follows, most often, Roger Sharrock, particularly for the imprisonments and the writing of *The Pilgrim's Progress,* Part I.

Chapter One

1. George Offor, ed., *The Works of John Bunyan* (Glasgow, 1858–59), II, 390. Hereafter cited as "Offor." This edition is used for all of Bunyan's works except *Grace Abounding, The Pilgrim's Progress,* and *A Book for Boys and Girls.*
2. Richard Greaves in his *John Bunyan* (Grand Rapids, Mich.; 1969) says that it is pointless to try to label Bunyan as a Baptist or Congregationalist because of his liberal views. Also, he is a *strict* rather than a *moderate* Calvinist, but he had some Antinomian leanings and was greatly influenced by Luther as well.
3. *Grace Abounding,* ed. Roger Sharrock (Oxford, 1962), p. 87. References for *Grace Abounding* are to this edition, hereafter cited as "Sharrock."
4. Offor, III, 419.
5. Offor, II, 538.
6. Offor, I, 68.
7. Bunyan's editor, Charles Doe, says that Bunyan wrote sixty works. However, *Reprobation Asserted* is considered repudiable (Harrison, pp. 34–35, n.).
8. For other accounts that fill out the biography of Bunyan, see chapter 8.
9. *A Relation of the Imprisonment of Mr. John Bunyan,* in Sharrock's edition of *Grace Abounding,* p. 124.
10. Ibid., p. 128.
11. Offor, I, 64*.
12. Harrison, pp. 13–15. The first edition is undated but was probably

published between 1660 and 1662.

13. Ibid., pp. 16–18.
14. Ibid., p. 26.
15. Ibid., pp. 26–27.
16. Ibid., pp. 32–33.
17. Extracts are given in appendix C of Sharrock's edition of *Grace Abounding*. G. B. Harrison edited in 1929 *A Narrative of the Persecution of Agnes Beaumont in the Year 1674*.
18. Harrison, pp. 33–35. No copy of *Peaceable Principles* is known.
19. No copy is known (Harrison, pp. 36–37).
20. Since Bedford had no ecclesiastical prison, Bunyan must have been sent again to the county jail, despite the legend that he spent one imprisonment in the town lockup over the Ouse. The story probably originated from the discovery of a gold ring inscribed "J. B." in the ruins of that building in 1811.
21. Harrison, p. 50.
22. An interesting example of how effective the Bunyan biography has been on others is to be found in Reginald L. Hine, *Confessions of an Uncommon Attorney* (New York, 1949), who tells, among numerous references to Bunyan, about how one of his clients found the anvil and fiddle and about the entry of Bunyan's name on the muster roll of the Newport Pagnell garrison.

Chapter Two

1. Sharrock, p. 62.
2. Ibid., p. 44.
3. William York Tindall, *John Bunyan: Mechanick Preacher* (New York, 1934; reprinted, 1964), p. 41, has beautifully summarized the relation of *Grace Abounding* to Bunyan's other works: "In one sense, *Grace Abounding*, which carried the exemplary burden of his evangelism, is the most significant book that Bunyan wrote, and his other books for the greater part but variant or ancillary expressions of its theme."

The relationships to *The Pilgrim's Progress* are especially numerous. During his "moral" conversion, Bunyan is very like Worldly Wiseman of the town of Carnal Policy and becomes a "brisk talker," setting the fashion for Talkative and Brisk. He hates hypocrisy; feels himself in a "miry bog," which corresponds to the Slough of Despond; encounters enumerable Giants Despair; talks of his "burden"; cannot tell whether he or the Devil speaks — like Christian in the Valley of the Shadow of Death; and ponders the "man among the tombs" (p. 58), the forerunner of the blind men seen by Christian and Hopeful from Mount Caution. Christian's running from his family is well provided for by Bunyan's inability to understand how "professors" (that is, those who "profess") of religion can be so cast down by such outward losses as husband, wife, or child; his assertion that the backsliding of one of those converted by his preaching is more to him than the death of one of his children; and his agreement with Matthew 10:37. On the other hand, in prison he feels that he is "somewhat too fond" of his family and is especially torn by leaving behind his blind daughter.

4. Critical controversy has tended to settle on the question of whether *Grace Abounding* is "truth" or "art." The consensus is that it is a sincere work but the product of a conscious or unconscious artist. An interesting treatment of its art form is Melvin R. Watson, "The Drama of *Grace Abounding,*" *English Studies,* 46 (1965), 471–82.

5. Sharrock, p. 11.

6. Robert Southey, in the life of Bunyan that prefaces his edition of *The Pilgrim's Progress,* was among the first to suggest that Bunyan was only a "blackguard" at most; and Thomas Babington Macaulay felt that even this was too great a censure.

7. Sharrock, p. 92.

8. William James, "The Divided Self, and the Process of Its Unification," in *The Varieties of Religious Experience* (New York, 1911), pp. 166–88. See also Josiah Royce, "The Case of John Bunyan," in *Studies of Good and Evil* (New York, 1898), pp. 29–75, for a psychological approach.

9. Most of Bunyan's works emphasize the faculties. In *Grace Abounding,* the memory receives especial emphasis in the preface; and Joan Webber, in "Donne and Bunyan: The Styles of Two Faiths," in *The Eloquent "I"* (Madison, 1968), pp. 15–52, feels that the whole work is a personal exercise in remembrance and is a tool to be used by others in their own memory exercises.

Bunyan worries about not being able to *hear, see, feel,* and *savor* Christ (Sharrock, p. 26) and is afflicted by the *sight* of his own wickedness. Sounding a note like the mystics' use of composition of place, he testifies to a sense of *seeing* the events of the life of Christ (p. 38) and many "golden Seals" of Christ's salvation (p. 40); and he sees with the "eyes of his soul" Jesus at God's right hand (p. 72). In a moment of happiness, he *sees* and *feels* Jesus. Cf. Sharrock in *John Bunyan* (London, 1954), who feels that images of the tactile sense predominate. The Puritan reliance on the aural sense is carried in *Grace Abounding* by the emphasis on preaching: the parson who speaks on Sabbath-breaking, Gifford, and Bunyan's own ministry to others.

10. Sharrock, *Grace Abounding,* p. 50. The remaining references to Sharrock in chapter 2 are to this edition of the autobiography.

11. Ibid., p. 40.

12. Ibid., p. 63. See Owen C. Watkins, *The Puritan Experience: Studies in Spiritual Autobiography* (New York, 1972), p. 110: "...the Scripture ... assumes the role of a protagonist with whom he argues and struggles and which has a complex life of its own."

13. Cf. Barrett John Mandel, "Bunyan and the Autobiographer's Artistic Purpose," *Criticism,* 10 (1968), 225–43: The main polarities are Satan and Bunyan, with God having a much lesser role.

14. Sharrock, p. 9.

15. Ibid., p. 31.

16. Ibid., p. 57.

17. Ibid., p. 53.

18. John N. Morris, "Religious Lives," in *Versions of the Self* (New York, 1966), p. 96.

19. Joan Webber, "Donne and Bunyan: The Styles of Two Faiths," in *The Eloquent "I."*

20. Sharrock, p. 28.

21. Ibid., p. 34.

22. Ibid., p. 26.

23. Ibid., p. 35.

24. Ibid., p. 15.

25. Ibid., p. 26.

26. Ibid., pp. 25–26.

27. Ibid., p. 33.

28. Ibid., pp. 60–61.

29. Ibid., p. 77.

30. Ibid., p. 78.

31. Ibid., p. 60.

32. Ibid., p. 78.

33. Ibid., p. 81.

34. Ibid., p. 53.

35. Ibid., p. 96.

36. Ibid., p. 64.

37. Ibid., p. 40.

Chapter Three

1. Sharrock, "John Bunyan: *The Pilgrim's Progress*," *Studies in English Literature,* no. 27 (London, 1966), p. 123.

2. Gordon Rupp, "John Bunyan and *Pilgrim's Progress,*" in *Six Makers of English Religion, 1500–1700* (London, 1957), p. 97.

3. J. W. Mackail, *The Pilgrim's Progress: A Lecture Delivered at the Royal Institution of Great Britain March 14, 1924* (London, 1924), p. 13.

4. H. E. Greene, "The Allegory as Employed by Spenser, Bunyan and Swift," *PMLA,* 4 (1889), 162.

5. Bunyan critics exhibit an almost universal feeling of dissatisfaction with the treatment Ignorance receives. Mackail feels that Bunyan is merciless to this character alone; and Alfred Noyes, in his vituperative "Bunyan — a Revaluation," *The Bookman,* 74 (1928), 13–17, reprinted in *The*

Opalescent Parrot (London, 1929), finds Ignorance one of the few "modest and true Christians" and lists him with Talkative and Atheist as almost the only "decent" characters; he is unable to fathom Bunyan's punishment of him. Others try to account for Bunyan's vehemence by the extent of Ignorance's crimes. For example, he is frequently associated with the Quaker reliance on the "inner light." John W. Draper, "Bunyan's Mr. Ignorance," *Modern Language Review,* 22 (1927), 15–21, associates him with the Deists or disciples of natural religion; and Sharrock (*John Bunyan: The Pilgrim's Progress*) suggests that he represents the Latitudinarian Anglican. Maurice Hussey, "Bunyan's Mr. Ignorance," *Modern Language Review,* 44 (1949), 483–89, finds him a hypocrite whose sins are carnal security and self-reliance. A similar view appears in James F. Forrest, "Bunyan's Ignorance and the Flatterer: A Study in the Literary Art of Damnation," *Studies in Philology,* 60 (1963), 12–22, who accuses Ignorance and certain other characters of a "narcissistic self-centeredness" and finds him relying on his own merits rather than on Christ. Ignorance and the Quaker, George Fox, both believe in the basic rightness of the human heart, according to Richard F. Hardin in "Bunyan, Mr. Ignorance, and the Quakers," *Studies in Philology,* 69 (1972), 496–508.

6. Mackail, *Studies in Humanism* (London, 1938), p. 157, suggests that Christian has a "museum headache."

7. John Livingston Lowes, "*The Pilgrim's Progress:* A Study in Literary Immortality," in *Essays in Appreciation* (Cambridge, Mass., 1936), p. 63.

8. Hussey, "Bunyan's Mr. Ignorance," p. 483.

9. A good presentation of the self-orientation of the characters is Stanley Eugene Fish, "Progress in *The Pilgrim's Progress,*" *English Literary Renaissance,* 1 (1971), 261–93.

10. Q. D. Leavis, "The Puritan Conscience," in *Fiction and the Reading Public* (London, 1932; reprinted 1965), p. 101, believes that the characteristic effect of reading a passage of Bunyan is a stirring of the blood in response to the accumulated religious associations of the race.

11. James Blanton Wharey, ed., *The Pilgrim's Progress from this World to That which is to Come,* 2d ed., rev. Roger Sharrock (Oxford, 1960), p. 44. References for *The Pilgrim's Progress* (Parts I and II) are to this edition, hereafter cited as "Wharey."

12. See Roland Mushat Frye, "*Pilgrim's Progress* and the Christian Life," in *God, Man, and Satan* (Princeton, 1960), pp. 95–167, for Bunyan's use of such symbols.

13. The emblems of *The Pilgrim's Progress,* Parts I and II, are discussed, with Bunyan's emblem book, in chapter 7.

14. Mabel Peacock, ed., *Bunyan: The Holy War and the Heavenly Foot-man* (Oxford, 1892), p. 296. In the Author's Apology prefacing Part I of *The Pilgrim's Progress,* Bunyan says that he was working on another

book when he suddenly fell into an allegory; Part I of *The Pilgrim's Progress* virtually demanded to be made into a separate work. At one time, critics identified the interrupted work as *The Strait Gate,* whose name has connections with the Wicket-gate, for example, and which provides sketches of different kinds of "professors" who run for heaven. More recently, however, *The Heavenly Foot-man* has been favored. In addition to the interest in Lot's wife, it cautions against bypaths and against keeping one's ear open to everything that calls, an apt gloss on Christian's fleeing with his fingers in his ears and on Christian and Faithful's stopping their ears in Vanity Fair.

15. Wharey, p. 99. It is interesting that By-ends and so many of the now famous moments and personages of the story were added in later editions. Among these additions are Christian's relation of his difficulties to his family, Worldly Wise-man and Christian's confession to Good-will that he was deceived by him, the discourse in the Palace Beautiful, Lot's wife, Despair's fits during bouts of the sun, Diffidence, and the identification of the "den" as "gaol" (the margin of the seventh edition).

16. Ibid., p. 77.

17. Ibid., p. 85.

18. Ibid., p. 128.

19. Fish, p. 278, suggests a pun on "sun" in the second part of the Valley of the Shadow of Death.

20. Wharey, p. 65.

21. Fish, pp. 281–82, considers memory the most important faculty of the work and identifies every crisis as one of memory.

22. Wharey, p. 161.

Chapter Four

1. The borrowing is my own, but Edward Dowden in "John Bunyan," *Puritan and Anglican: Studies in Literature,* 2d ed. (New York, 1901), p. 256, has linked *The Life and Death of Mr. Badman* with William Hogarth, calling it a "bourgeois Rake's Progress"; and G. B. Harrison, *John Bunyan, a Study in Personality* (Hamden, Conn., 1967), p. 153, describes it as the "Puritan answer to the rake."

2. This is a slip by Bunyan since he initially reported that the bell tolled for Badman "yesterday." The "stinking" is part of the paraphernalia of punishment used to such advantage in Shakespeare's *Pericles* and in the legends surrounding Antiochus and his daughters from which the play was woven. Several of the anecdotes that Bunyan borrows from Samuel Clark's *Mirrour for Saints and Sinners* involve similar phenomena. Two adulterers are struck dead by fire from heaven, and their bodies give out a loathsome "savor." A drunkard in a tavern drinks to the health of the Devil and dares him to return the pledge; the vintner hears a noise and smells a stink; the man disappears.

3. For a discussion of the likenesses, see Wharey, "Bunyan's *Mr. Badman,*" *Modern Language Notes,* 36 (1921), 65–79. He does not point out the initial references of both to cows.

4. The relationship of *Badman* to the "literature of judgment" is discussed in Maurice Hussey, "John Bunyan and the Books of God's Judgements: A Study of . . . *Badman,*" *English,* 7 (1949), 165–67.

5. Jack Lindsay, *John Bunyan, Maker of Myths* (Port Washington, N.Y., 1937; reprinted 1969), p. 209.

6. Hussey, "Arthur Dent's *Plaine Mans Path-Way to Heaven,*" *Modern Language Review,* 44 (1949), 33. Sharrock (*John Bunyan,* p. 116) sees it as Bunyan's nearest approach to the novel.

7. L. D. Lerner, "Bunyan and the Puritan Culture," *Cambridge Journal,* 7 (1954), 226.

8. While this satire of the times is a standard feature of Bunyan's works, it is difficult to agree with Offor and other earlier critics that Bunyan was frequently in danger from the authorities for his political diatribes. His denunciations remain largely biblical and generalized.

9. Offor, III, 621.

10. For example, Augustine Birrell, "John Bunyan," *The Bookman,* 73 (1927), 147–52.

11. George Bernard Shaw, *Everybody's Political What's What?* and elsewhere. Several critics have been interested in Shaw's admiration for Bunyan: Norbert F. O'Donnell, "Shaw, Bunyan, and Puritanism," *PMLA,* 72 (1957), 520–33; E. E. Stokes, Jr., "Bernard Shaw's Debt to John Bunyan," *Shaw Review,* 8 (1965), 42–51; and Scott McMillin, "G. B. S. and Bunyan's *Badman,*" *Shaw Review,* 9 (1966), 90–101. Von Wolfgang Sachs, *Der typisch puritanische Ideengehalt in Bunyan's Life and Death of Mr. Badman* (Leipzig, 1936), opposes the view that modern capitalism can see its roots in Bunyan's work.

12. Offor, III, 601.

13. Ibid., p. 610.

14. The spider is discussed in chapter 7.

15. Offor, III, 602.

16. Ibid., p. 607.

17. If Wiseman is Bunyan, the strangest portion of *Badman* is the story of the man who told his drab that, if she became pregnant, she could escape punishment by saying that her partner was the Holy Ghost. Wiseman admits that he should have accused this man before the magistrates; but, since the culprit was well-known and moneyed and since Wiseman was poor and young, he did not report the case!

18. Offor, III, 645.

19. Ibid., p. 695.

20. Ibid., p. 711.

21. For Bunyan's development of the Dorothy Mately story, which he found in Clark, see Hussey, "John Bunyan and the Books of God's

Judgements...."

22. Offor, III, 611.

23. Ola Elizabeth Winslow, *John Bunyan* (New York, 1961), p. 171, identifies "W. S." as William Swinton of Bedford, the sexton of St. Cuthbert's Church.

Chapter Five

1. Thomas Babington Macaulay, "John Bunyan," *Critical, Historical, and Miscellaneous Essays and Poems* (New York, n.d.), III, 263.

2. Offor, I, lxx, lxxi.

3. G. B. Harrison, *John Bunyan, A Study in Personality,* p. 168.

4. For example, Paul Elmer More, "Bunyan," in *Shelburne Essays* (New York, 1909), p. 210. Harrison, *John Bunyan, A Study in Personality,* p. 167, also finds confusion: Mansoul is sometimes the people and sometimes the town.

5. Greene, p. 163, finds it to be conducted primarily by personifications acting in accordance with their names.

6. Shaw, in the preface to *Androcles and the Lion.*

7. Sharrock (*John Bunyan,* p. 121) especially promotes *Paradise Lost,* for he thinks that perhaps one of Bunyan's more learned friends introduced him to it. Many of the doctrinal features and artifices, such as the infernal councils, do show obvious relations. Two more subtle examples, though one would not insist upon influence, are the treatment of the hunger of hell and the humor of the episodes between Profane and Cerberus, which parallel that of the "allegorical" scenes of Satan, Sin, and Death in *Paradise Lost.* The ravenousness of Death is matched by Diabolus' appointment of Captain Insatiable and by this description of hell's inhabitants: "...their raging gorge thought everyday even as long as a short-for-ever, until they were filled with the body and soul, with the flesh and bones, and with all the delicates of Mansoul" (Offor, III, 361). Bunyan is also similar to Milton in having evil parody good, as in Diabolus' arming of the Mansoulians, hell's rejoicing after the manner of heaven but ringing Deadman's Bell instead of sounding trumpets, and Diabolus' setting up mountains around Mansoul that mimic those of Shaddai. Perhaps parodic, too, is the fact that many of the Diabolonians are crucified. Finally, Bunyan seems to suggest the *felix culpa* (which critics often assume that Milton believes in) when God promises to put Mansoul in a "far better and more happy condition" than before the takeover by Diabolus.

8. Wharey, *A Study of the Sources of Bunyan's Allegories* (Baltimore, 1904), believes that Bunyan was probably familiar with *The Isle of Man* and that it induced him to write *The Holy War.* Cf. Richard Heath, "The Archetype of *The Holy War,*" *The Contemporary Review,* 72 (1897),

105-18, who feels that Bunyan was mirroring the history of the Münster Anabaptist struggle (1534-1536).

9. There are, indeed, many technical links with *The Pilgrim's Progress,* Part I. The opening, if it cannot quite match the beauty of the first lines of the earlier work, does catch its rhythm. (Cf. Winslow, who links the beginning of *The Holy War* with current Utopias.) The terms *den* and *maul* recur and shed more light on the den/gaol and the Giant Maul of *The Pilgrim's Progress.* The trial scenes recall that of Faithful and are quite as circumstantial as his. Apollyon becomes one of Diabolus' henchmen, and Bunyan spends some time correcting our views as he locates the Land of Doubting between Darkness and the Valley of the Shadow of Death. Diabolus' arming of his men is a parody of the breastplate of righteousness and of the arming of Christian in the Palace Beautiful.

10. Offor, III, 320.

11. Ibid., p. 257.

12. Tindall, *John Bunyan: Mechanick Preacher,* chap. 7, pp. 144-65.

13. Sharrock, *John Bunyan,* p. 126.

14. Lindsay, p. 216.

15. Offor, III, 293.

16. E.M.W. Tillyard, *The English Epic and Its Background* (London, 1954), p. 406.

17. Offor, III, 265.

18. Ibid., p. 265.

19. Ibid., p. 557. Offor points out that "is proved" was commonly used in advertising medical prescriptions and that Bunyan's use of *aquae vitae* in this same prose work came from the name of a popular cordial water. In the margin of *The Pilgrim's Progress,* Part II, Bunyan admits that he "borrows the Lattine" for *ex Carne & Sanguine Christi.*

20. Ibid., p. 268.

21. Ibid., p. 288.

22. Ibid., p. 293.

23. Ibid., p. 260.

24. Ibid., p. 256.

25. Ibid., pp. 261, 267.

26. Ibid., p. 267, a marginal comment.

27. Ibid., p. 340.

Chapter Six

1. Henri Talon, *John Bunyan, The Man and His Works* (Paris, 1948), trans. Barbara Wall (Cambridge, Mass., 1951), pp. 103-5.

2. Sharrock, ed., *The Pilgrim's Progress from this World to That which is to Come,* p. 352. Bunyan also used the funereal imagery of Ecclesiastes in his series of four poems, *One Thing Is Needful.*

3. Wharey, p. 74.

4. Ibid., pp. 183–84.

5. Ibid., p. 301.

6. Ibid., p. 219.

7. One is surprised by the tendency of critics to ignore this conclusion, but Bunyan is quite specific (Wharey, pp. 194–95) and makes a more general reference to the same situation in *The Holy War.*

8. Wharey, p. 268.

9. Ibid., p. 223.

10. Ibid., p. 288, my italics. Sharrock, in *John Bunyan,* p. 146, points out that there is a pun in the gripes episode on "Matthew's powders," a universal remedy of the Restoration period.

11. Wharey, p. 253.

12. Ibid., p. 238.

13. Mackail, *Studies in Humanism,* p. 161.

14. Wharey, p. 295.

15. See chapter 7 for a discussion of the emblems (symbolic pictures) in *The Pilgrim's Progress.*

16. Alison White, *"Pilgrim's Progress* as a Fairy-Tale," *Children's Literature,* 1 (1972), 42–45.

17. Wharey, p. 51.

18. Ibid., p. 52.

19. Ibid., p. 261.

20. Ibid., p. 182.

21. Ibid., p. 196.

22. Ibid., p. 202.

23. Ibid., p. 190.

24. Sharrock, *John Bunyan: The Pilgrim's Progress,* pp. 149–50.

25. Rosemary Freeman, "John Bunyan: The End of the Tradition," in *English Emblem Books* (London, 1948; reprinted New York, 1970), pp. 224–25.

26. Wharey, p. 214.

Chapter Seven

1. Freeman, "John Bunyan: The End of the Tradition," in *English Emblem Books,* p. 212.

2. Offor reprints one of the reduced editions that includes only forty-nine emblems. The most convenient modern edition, consulted here, is E. S. Buchanan, ed., *John Bunyan, A Book for Boys and Girls* (New York, 1928). John Brown edited a facsimile of the first edition in 1889.

3. Offor, II, 568.

4. Quarles and Dent are the most frequently cited influences on the Muckraker, but it is also similar to the "thing armed with a rake" that the Cardinal sees in John Webster's *The Duchess of Malfi.*

Notes and References

149

5. Buchanan, Introduction, *John Bunyan, A Book for Boys and Girls.*

6. See Freeman, p. 212.

7. For extensive treatment, see U. Milo Kaufmann, *The Pilgrim's Progress and Traditions in Puritan Meditation* (New Haven, 1966), p. 194.

8. Offor, II, 111.

9. F. J. Harvey Darton, "The Puritans: 'Good Godly Books,' " in *Children's Books in England: Five Centuries of Social Life* (Cambridge, England, 1932; reprinted 1966), p. 67.

10. Alfred Noyes, in *The Opalescent Parrot,* pp. 90–91, finds the spider emblem "One of the most horrible things ever printed" and sees Bunyan and the Interpreter indulging in "disgusting male bullying."

11. Kaufman, p. 62.

12. Offor, I, 435.

13. Ibid., p. 396.

14. Ibid., III, 600.

15. Ibid., I, 732.

16. Ibid., II, 390.

17. On the dramatic quality of the emblems, see Kaufman, especially chapter 4.

18. The term is Sharrock's in "Bunyan and the English Emblem Writers," *Review of English Studies,* 21 (1945), 105–16.

19. David J. Alpaugh, "Emblem and Interpretation in *The Pilgrim's Progress,*" *Journal of English Literary History,* 33 (1966), 299–324, provides a good account of how Bunyan's use of the emblem is bound up with the illumination and interpretation of experience.

20. Kaufman places the emblems within the tradition of Puritan practices of meditation. Bunyan uses the term *meditation* in the titles of his poem, *One Thing Is Needful; Or, Serious Meditations Upon the Four Last Things* (ca. 1665), and of his prose work, *Profitable Meditations* (1661).

21. Offor, I, 647. Offor's queries about the riddlelike qualities of the passage appear in his "Memoir of John Bunyan," *Works,* I, lxxviii.

Chapter Eight

1. Mackail, *Studies in Humanism,* p. 151.

2. In *A Letter to a Young Gentleman,* Jonathan Swift proclaims that he has been "better entertained and more informed by a Chapter in the *Pilgrim's Progress,* than by a long Discourse upon the *Will* and the *Intellect,* and *simple* or *complex* Ideas." Calhoun Winton, "Conversion on the Road to Houyhnhnmland," *Sewanee Review,* 68 (1960), 20–33, suggests that *Gulliver's Travels* intentionally echoes *The Pilgrim's Progress.*

3. White also provided the only full-length figure of Bunyan for the first edition of *The Holy War.* Other contemporary portraits are the oil picture by Thomas Sadler (1685) and the engraving by John Sturt (1692).

Reportedly, a 1673 portrait by an unknown artist was acquired by the father of Robert L. Stevenson and was carried by the son to Samoa as a prized possession. Stevenson especially liked the illustrations of *The Pilgrim's Progress* by Eunice Bagster and her brother. He listed this work as one of the books that influenced him, and he felt that Christian's running with his fingers in his ears was a "culminating moment" "printed on the mind's eye forever." He likened the "allegories" of the Interpreter and the Shepherds to stage plays but also recognized some inconsistencies in the work.

4. Alison White draws interesting parallels between *The Pilgrim's Progress* and works of both Tolkien and Homer.

5. Mark Twain subtitles another work after Bunyan — *The Innocents Abroad or The New Pilgrims' Progress Being Some Account of the Steamship Quaker City's Pleasure Excursion to Europe and the Holy Land.*

6. Of the "allegorical" works after Bunyan, Maurice Hussey, in "The Humanism of John Bunyan," *From Donne to Marvell* (Aylesbury, Bucks, England, 1956), pp. 219–32, *The Pelican Guide to English Literature,* vol. 3, places directly in Bunyan's tradition Hawthorne's *The Scarlet Letter, The Blithedale Romance,* and "Young Goodman Brown"; Melville's *Benito Cereno* and *Billy Budd;* and T. F. Powys': *Mr. Weston's Good Wine.*

7. For accounts of Bunyan's influence on Hawthorne, see Hussey, "The Humanism of John Bunyan"; W. Stacy Johnson, "Hawthorne and *The Pilgrim's Progress,"* *Journal of English and Germanic Philology,* 50 (1951), 156–66; Sacvan Bercovitch, "Diabolus in Salem," *English Language Notes,* 6 (1969), 280–85; and David E. Smith, *John Bunyan in America* (Bloomington, 1966).

8. See Bercovitch.

9. J. B. Grier, *Studies in the English of Bunyan* (Philadelphia, 1872).

10. Richard Winboult Harding, *John Bunyan: His Life and Times* (London, 1928), p. 89. For other Indian influence, see D. Yesudhas, *"The Pilgrim's Progress* and *Iratciniya Yaattirikam,"* *Proceedings of the First International Conference Seminar of Tamil Studies,* ed. Thani Nayagam et al. (Kuala Lumpur, 1968–1969), II, 232–36. See Brown's appendices for just a few of the many translations, adaptations, etc.

11. Paul Kaufman, "Revelation by Subscribers: John Bunyan among the Welsh," *Library Review,* 21 (1968), 227–29.

12. See Smith, *John Bunyan in America;* and Kenneth Walter Cameron, "Bunyan and the Writers of the American Renaissance," *American Transcendental Quarterly,* 13-(1972), supple. pt. 1, pp. 1–47.

13. See Smith, "Illustrations of American Editions of *The Pilgrim's Progress* to 1870," *Princeton University Library Chronicle,* Autumn, *Chronicle,* 26 (1964), 16–25. For English illustrations, see Frank Mott Harrison, "Some Illustrators of *The Pilgrim's Progress* (Part One): John Bunyan," *The Library,* 17 (1936), 241–63.

14. See Smith, *John Bunyan in America;* George H. Williams, *Wilderness and Paradise in Christian Thought* (New York, 1962); and Charles L. Sanford, *The Quest for Paradise* (Urbana, 1961).

15. Frank Luther Mott, *Golden Multitudes: The Story of Best Sellers in the United States* (New York, 1947), pp. 19-20.

16. See Smith, *"The Enormous Room* and *The Pilgrim's Progress,"* *Twentieth Century Literature,* 11 (1965), 67-75; and Kingsley Widmer, "Timeless Prose," *Twentieth Century Literature,* 4 (1958), 3-8.

17. Ronald A. Knox, "The Identity of the Pseudo-Bunyan," *Essays in Satire* (London, 1928), pp. 136-50.

18. James Joyce, *Ulysses* (New York, 1934), p. 389. The parody is also pointed out in Dwight Macdonald, ed., *Parodies: An Anthology from Chaucer to Beerbohm — and After* (New York, 1960).

Selected Bibliography

PRIMARY SOURCES

1. Collected editions

DOE, CHARLES. *The Works of ... Mr. John Bunyan....* London: William Marshall, 1692. A one-volume folio, including ten previously unpublished works whose manuscripts Doe secured from Mrs. Bunyan.

The Miscellaneous Works of John Bunyan. New York: Oxford University Press, 1976- . Thirteen volumes projected. Based on the earliest editions and on Doe's folio. Three volumes currently published.

OFFOR, GEORGE. *The Works of John Bunyan.* 3 vols. Glasgow: Blackie and Son, 1858–1859. The standard edition.

STEBBING, H[ENRY]. *The Entire Works of John Bunyan.* 4 vols. London: James S. Virtue, 1859–1860.

2. Editions of individual works

BROWN, JOHN, ed. *A Book for Boys and Girls: or, Country Rhymes for Children.* London: Elliot Stock, 1889. A facsimile of the first edition.

————, ed. *The Life and Death of Mr. Badman and The Holy War.* Cambridge: Cambridge University Press, 1905.

BUCHANAN, E. S., ed. *John Bunyan, A Book for Boys and Girls Or Country Rhymes for Children.* New York: American Tract Society, 1928. Most readily available modern edition.

BURDER, GEORGE, ed. *The Holy War.* Philadelphia: Presbyterian Board of Publication, 1803. Noted for its illustrations.

FORREST, JAMES F., ed. *The Holy War.* New York: New York University Press, 1967. The most accessible modern edition.

HARRISON, G. B., ed. *The Life and Death of Mr. Badman.* World's Classics. Oxford: Oxford University Press, 1929.

————, ed. *Grace Abounding and The Life and Death of Mr. Badman.* Everyman's Library. London: J. M. Dent & Sons, 1928.

PEACOCK, MABEL, ed. *Bunyan: The Holy War and the Heavenly Foot-Man.* Oxford: Clarendon Press, 1892.

SHARROCK, ROGER, ed. *Grace Abounding to the Chief of Sinners.* Oxford: Clarendon Press, 1962. The standard edition.

TALON, HENRI A., ed. *God's Knotty Log: Selected Writings of John Bun-*

yan. Meridian Books. Cleveland: The World Publishing Company, 1961. Includes *The Heavenly Foot-man.* Introduction suggests that Talon's earlier work stressed too heavily Bunyan's background and the realism of some secondary characters in *The Pilgrim's Progress.*

WHAREY, JAMES BLANTON, ed. *The Pilgrim's Progress.* . . . 2d ed. Revised by Roger Sharrock. Oxford: Clarendon Press, 1960. The standard edition.

3. Bibliographical

HARRISON, FRANK MOTT. *A Bibliography of the Works of John Bunyan.* Bibliographical Society. Oxford: Oxford University Press, 1932.

SECONDARY SOURCES

1. General works

BRITTAIN, VERA. *In the Steps of John Bunyan: An Excursion into Puritan England.* London: Rich and Cowan, [1950]. Relates people and events in *The Pilgrim's Progress* to Bedfordshire.

BROWN, JOHN. *John Bunyan (1628–1688): His Life, Times, and Work.* London, 1855. Revised by Frank Mott Harrison. London: Marshall, Morgan and Scott, 1928. Still the standard biography.

DOWDEN, EDWARD. "John Bunyan." In *Puritan and Anglican: Studies in Literature.* 2d ed. New York: Henry Holt, 1901. Pp. 232–78. Presents a solid account; author stresses Bunyan as the product of Puritanism.

FIRTH, SIR CHARLES. "John Bunyan." In *Essays Historical and Literary.* Oxford: Clarendon Press, 1938. Pp. 129–73. Much on the parallels between Bunyan's works and popular romances.

FROUDE, JAMES ANTHONY. *Bunyan.* Men of Letters Series. New York: Harper, 1880. Somewhat dated.

GLOVER, T. R. "Bunyan." In *Poets and Puritans.* London: Methuen, 1915. Good on relating Bunyan to his milieu.

GODBER, JOYCE. "The Imprisonments of John Bunyan," *Transactions of the Congregational Historical Society,* 16 (1949), 23–32. Essential.

GREAVES, RICHARD LEE. *John Bunyan.* Courtenay Studies in Reformation Theology, vol. 2. Grand Rapids, Mich.: William B. Eerdmans Publishing Company, 1969. On Bunyan's theology. Useful glossary.

GREENE, HERBERT EVELETH. "The Allegory as Employed by Spenser, Bunyan and Swift." *PMLA,* 4 (1889), 145–93. Bunyan succeeds because he is not a perfect allegorist.

HARRISON, G. B. *John Bunyan, a Study in Personality.* London: J. M. Dent and Sons, 1928. Essential. Very readable. Close analysis of many minor works.

————, ed. *The Church Book of Bunyan Meeting 1650–1821.* London: J. M. Dent and Sons, 1928. Useful for revealing Bunyan's activities

HILL, CHRISTOPHER. "Milton and Bunyan: Dialogue with the Radicals." In *The World Turned Upside Down: Radical Ideas During the English Revolution.* London: Temple Smith, 1972. Appendix 2, pp. 320–36. Bunyan shared the social and political attitudes of the radicals but not their theology.

HUSSEY, MAURICE. "The Humanism of John Bunyan." In *The Pelican Guide to English Literature,* vol. 3, *From Donne to Marvell.* Aylesbury, Bucks, England: Haxell Watson & Viney, 1956. Pp. 219–32. An excellent, essential view.

KNOX, EDMUND ARBUTHNOTT. *John Bunyan in Relation to His Times.* London, New York: Longmans, Green, 1928. A very full account of Bunyan's religion and period.

KOLLER, KATHRINE. "The Puritan Preacher's Contribution to Fiction." *Huntington Library Quarterly,* 11 (1948), 321–40. Puritan sermons influenced Bunyan's use of dialogue and handling of despair.

LERNER, L. D. "Bunyan and the Puritan Culture." *Cambridge Journal,* 7 (1954), 221–42. pp. 221–42. Examines Puritanism to interpret Bunyan's works.

LINDSAY, JACK. *John Bunyan, Maker of Myths.* London: Metheun, 1937. Emphasizes both the social forces influencing Bunyan and his "mythmaking faculties." Often referred to as Marxist criticism.

MORE, PAUL ELMER. "Bunyan." In *Shelburne Essays.* 6th ser. New York: G. P. Putnam, 1909. Pp. 187–213. A basic study.

OWST, G[ERALD] R. *Literature and Pulpit in Medieval England.* 2d ed. rev. Oxford: Basil Blackwell, 1961. Sees links between Bunyan's major works and Medieval materials and themes.

SHARROCK, ROGER. *John Bunyan.* London: Hutchinson's University Library, 1954. A lucid and good biography by one of the best Bunyan critics.

————. "The Origin of *A Relation of the Imprisonment of Mr. John Bunyan.*" *Review of English Studies,* n.s., 10 (1959), 250–56. Information about a work not published until 1765.

SMITH, DAVID E. *John Bunyan in America.* Bloomington: Indiana University Press, 1966. Useful for Bunyan's influence.

TALON, HENRI ANTOINE. *John Bunyan, The Man and His Works.* Translated by Barbara Wall. Cambridge: Harvard University Press, 1951. A minute and impressive and very scholarly work.

TINDALL, WILLIAM YORK. *John Bunyan: Mechanick Preacher.* New York: Russell and Russell, 1934. Focused critical attention on Bunyan's milieu.

WHAREY, JAMES BLANTON. *A Study of the Sources of Bunyan's Allegories with Special Reference to Deguileville's Pilgrimage of Man.* Baltimore: J. H. Furst Company, 1904. Bernard's *Isle of Man* influenced *The Holy War.*

WINSLOW, OLA ELIZABETH. *John Bunyan.* New York: Macmillan, 1961. Sharrock suggests that this study supersedes that of Brown.

2. *Grace Abounding*

BOTTRALL, MARGARET. "Bunyan's *Grace Abounding.*" In *Every Man a Phoenix; Studies in Seventeenth-Century Autobiography.* London: John Murray, 1958. Pp. 82–110. A full and essential account.

HARRISON, FRANK MOTT. "Notes on the Early Editions of *Grace Abounding.*" *The Baptist Quarterly,* 11 (1943), 160–64. For the Bunyan scholar.

JAMES, WILLIAM. "The Divided Self, and the Process of Its Unification." In *The Varieties of Religious Experience: A Study in Human Nature.* New York: Longmans, Green, 1911. Pp. 166–88. About *Grace Abounding.*

LERNER, L. D. "Puritanism and the Spiritual Autobiography." *The Hibbert Journal,* 55 (1956–1957), 373–86. Relates *Grace Abounding* to the Puritan pattern of conversion.

MANDEL, BARRETT JOHN. "Bunyan and the Autobiographer's Artistic Purpose." *Criticism,* 10 (1968), 225–43. *Grace Abounding* as an artistic work.

MORRIS, JOHN N. "John Bunyan and the Head of Goliath." *South Atlantic Quarterly,* 64 (1965), 15–26. Especially good on the analytic tone of *Grace Abounding.* Reworked in *Versions of the Self: Studies in English Autobiography from John Bunyan to John Stuart Mill* (New York: Basic Books, 1966).

PASCAL, ROY. *Design and Truth in Autobiography.* Cambridge: Harvard University Press, 1960. Pp. 33–34. About Bunyan's candor and simplicity.

ROYCE, JOSIAH. "The Case of John Bunyan." In *Studies of Good and Evil: A Series of Essays Upon Problems of Philosophy and of Life.* New York: D. Appleton, 1898. Pp. 29–75. Good on the stages of Bunyan's "malady" and on his motor-speech functions and aural sense.

WATKINS, OWEN C. "Bunyan's *Grace Abounding.*" In *The Puritan Experience: Studies in Spiritual Autobiography.* New York: Schocken Books, 1972. Pp. 101–20. An important work. Especially good on Bunyan's use of language for dramatic ends.

WATSON, MELVIN R. "The Drama of *Grace Abounding.*" *English Studies,* 46 (1965), 471–82. A sound appraisal of *Grace Abounding* as a work of art.

WEBBER, JOAN. "Donne and Bunyan: The Styles of Two Faiths." In *The Eloquent "I": Style and Self in Seventeenth-Century Prose.* Madison: The University of Wisconsin Press, 1968. Pp. 15–52. An excellent criticism; underscores the importance of the faculties in *Grace Abounding.*

156 JOHN BUNYAN

3. *The Pilgrim's Progress*

ALPAUGH, DAVID J. "Emblem and Interpretation in *The Pilgrim's Progress.*" *Journal of English Literary History,* 33 (1966), 299–314. An important study of Bunyan's emblem technique.

DRAPER, JOHN W. "Bunyan's Mr. Ignorance." *Modern Language Review,* 22 (1927), 15–21. Relates Ignorance to the Deists and, to a lesser extent, to the Quakers.

FISH, STANLEY EUGENE. "Progress in *The Pilgrim's Progress.*" *English Literary Renaissance,* 1 (1971), 261–93. A valuable essay on how "progress" is bound up with the faculties. Revised in *Self-Consuming Artifacts: The Experience of Seventeenth-Century Literature* (Berkeley: University of California Press, 1972), pp. 224–64.

FORREST, JAMES F. "Bunyan's Ignorance and the Flatterer: A Study in the Literary Art of Damnation." *Studies in Philology,* 60 (1963), 12–22. A justification for Bunyan's treatment of Ignorance in terms of Bunyan's religious views. A fine article.

———. "Mercy with Her Mirror." *Philological Quarterly,* 42 (1963), 121–26. The iconography of the mirror, its use by the Puritans, and its connection with humility. An important study.

FRYE, ROLAND MUSHAT. "*Pilgrim's Progress* and the Christian Life." In *God, Man, and Satan: Patterns of Christian Thought in Paradise Lost, Pilgrim's Progress, and the Great Theologians.* Princeton: Princeton University Press, 1960. Pp. 95–167. Presents the doctrinal meaning of Bunyan's symbols and offers new insight into Bunyan's approach to Scripture.

GIBSON, DANIEL, JR. "On the Genesis of *Pilgrim's Progress.*" *Modern Philology,* 32 (1935), 365–82. *Grace Abounding, The Heavenly Footman,* and *The Strait-Gate* as preparations for *The Pilgrim's Progress.*

GOLDER, HAROLD. "Bunyan and Spenser." *PMLA,* 45 (1930), 216–37. Influence of Spenser on Bunyan is unlikely but possible.

———. "Bunyan's Giant Despair." *Journal of English and Germanic Philology,* 30 (1931), 361–78. Examines medical and religious tracts and popular tales originating in northern Germany as backgrounds for Bunyan's handling of despair.

———. "Bunyan's Hypocrisy." *North American Review,* 223 (1926), 323–32. Bunyan an hypocrite because he condemned the literature of romance and chivalry and yet obviously read it.

———. "Bunyan's Valley of the Shadow." *Modern Philology,* 27 (1929), 55–72. Influence of chivalric romance and, to a lesser extent, the Bible on Bunyan's valleys.

HARDIN, RICHARD F. "Bunyan, Mr. Ignorance, and the Quakers." *Studies in Philology,* 69 (1972), 496–508. Ignorance and George Fox both believe in the basic rightness of the human heart.

HARDING, MARY ESTHER. *Journey into Self.* New York: Longmans Green, 1956. A psychoanalytic analysis of *The Pilgrim's Progress* dedicated to Karl Jung.

HONIG, EDWIN. *Dark Conceit: the Making of Allegory.* Evanston: Northwestern University Press, 1959. Brief comments but good on the levels of allegory in *The Pilgrim's Progress.*

HUSSEY, MAURICE. "Bunyan's Mr. Ignorance." *Modern Language Review,* 44 (1949), 483–89. A justification of the treatment of Ignorance as related to carnal security.

KAUFMANN, U. MILO. *The Pilgrim's Progress and Traditions in Puritan Meditation.* New Haven: Yale University Press, 1966. One of the most scholarly and valuable recent commentaries.

KNOTT, JOHN R., JR. "Bunyan's Gospel Day: A Reading of *The Pilgrim's Progress.*" *English Literary Renaissance,* 3 (1973), 443–61. Good on Bunyan's use of the figurative language of the Bible based on Exodus and learned from Hebrews.

LEAVIS, F. R. "Bunyan Through Modern Eyes." In *The Common Pursuit.* London: Chatto and Windus, 1962. Pp. 204–10. Bunyan's great humanity in *The Pilgrim's Progress.*

LEAVIS, Q. D. "The Puritan Conscience." In *Fiction and the Reading Public.* London: Chatto and Windus, 1932; reprinted 1965. Pp. 97–117. The influence of the Puritan culture on *The Pilgrim's Progress.* An important criticism.

LOWES, JOHN LIVINGSTON. *"The Pilgrim's Progress:* A Study in Literary Immortality." In *Essays in Appreciation.* Cambridge, Mass.: The Riverside Press, 1936. Pp. 35–74. An overwhelmingly favorable account.

MACAULAY, THOMAS BABINGTON. "Southey's Edition of *The Pilgrim's Progress.*" In *Critical, Historical, and Miscellaneous Essays and Poems.* New York: John W. Lovell, n.d. I, 558–70. Also, "John Bunyan," III, 253–66. Originally published as "John Bunyan," *Edinburgh Review* (December, 1830). Necessary reading for Bunyan critics.

MACKAIL, J. W. *The Pilgrim's Progress: A Lecture Delivered at the Royal Institution of Great Britain March 14, 1924.* London: Longmans, Green, 1924. Excellent, though displays some tendency to overpraise. Also in *Studies in Humanism* (London: Longmans, Green, 1938), pp. 144–68.

NOYES, ALFRED. "Bunyan — a Revaluation." *The Bookman,* 74 (1928), 13–17. The one diatribe among tercentenary celebrations of Bunyan. Also in *The Opalescent Parrot: Essays* (London: Sheed and Ward, 1929), pp. 71–106.

PASCAL, ROY. "The Present Tense in *The Pilgrim's Progress.*" *Modern Language Review,* 60 (1965), 13–16. An interesting presentation of Bunyan's use of tenses to help distinguish Parts I and II.

REEVES, PASCHAL. *"The Pilgrim's Progress* as a Precursor of the Novel." *Georgia Review,* 20 (1966), 64–71. Does not insist that the novel could

not have developed without Bunyan. A levelheaded account of ways
he might have assisted its growth.

RUPP, GORDON. "John Bunyan and *Pilgrim's Progress.*" In *Six Makers of
English Religion, 1500–1700.* London: Hodder and Stoughton, 1957.
Pp. 92–101. Mostly on the relevance of the work to modern man.

SHARROCK, ROGER. "Bunyan and the English Emblem Writers." *Review
of English Studies,* 21 (1945), 105–16. The emblems not only provide
breaks in the narration but emphasize the necessity for close reading.

————. *John Bunyan: The Pilgrim's Progress.* Studies in English Literature Series, no. 27. London: Edward Arnold, 1966. A concise
account. Opposes the view that the only influence on Bunyan was the
Authorized Version of the Bible.

————. "Personal Vision and Puritan Tradition in Bunyan." *The Hibbert
Journal,* 56 (1957), 47–60. A plea for a middle-ground approach
between the views of Bunyan as a total individualist and of him as
merely part of a tradition.

————. "Spiritual Autobiography in *The Pilgrim's Progress.*" *Review of
English Studies,* 24 (1948), 102–20. The Calvinist basis of the work.

TALON, HENRI A. "Space and the Hero in *The Pilgrim's Progress:* A
Study of the Meaning of the Allegorical Universe." *Études Anglaises,*
14 (1961). 124–30. From his introduction to *God's Knotty Log.*

VAN GHENT, DOROTHY. "On *The Pilgrim's Progress.*" In *The English
Novel: Form and Function.* New York: Rinehart, 1953. Pp. 21–32.
Notably good on the fusion of realism with allegory and on the use
of topography.

4. *The Life and Death of Mr. Badman*

HUSSEY, MAURICE. "Arthur Dent's *Plaine Mans Path-Way to Heaven.*"
Modern Language Review, 44 (1949), 26–34. Dent's influence on
Badman. Basic to any study of the work.

————. "John Bunyan and the Books of God's Judgements: A Study of
The Life and Death of Mr. Badman." *English,* 7 (1949), 165–67. The
influence of judgment literature on *Badman.* Basic to any study of the
work.

MCMILLIN, SCOTT. "G. B. S. and Bunyan's *Badman.*" *Shaw Review,* 9
(1966), 90–101. The modernity of *Badman* from Shaw's point of
view.

WHAREY, JAMES BLANTON. "Bunyan's *Mr. Badman.*" *Modern Language
Notes,* 36 (1921), 65–79. Influence of Dent on *Badman.*

5. *The Holy War*

FIRTH, CHARLES H. "Bunyan's *Holy War.*" *The Journal of English
Studies,* 1 (1913), 141–50. One of the best treatments of this work.

HEATH, RICHARD. "The Archetype of *The Holy War.*" *The Contem-*

porary Review, 72 (1897), 105–18. Relates *The Holy War* to the history of the Anabaptist struggle in Münster, 1534–1536.

6. *A Book for Boys and Girls*

DARTON, F. J. HARVEY. "The Puritans: 'Good Godly Books.' " In *Children's Books in England: Five Centuries of Social Life.* 2d ed. Cambridge: Cambridge University Press, 1966. Pp. 53–69. Not very flattering to Bunyan. Sees him almost torturing his mind to find a moral in the emblems.

FREEMAN, ROSEMARY. "John Bunyan: The End of the Tradition." In *English Emblem Books.* London: Chatto and Windus, 1948. Pp. 204–28. A valuable essay; also covers the emblems of *The Pilgrim's Progress.* Essential reading.

Index

Index

163

Middleton, Thomas, 68
millenarianism, 19, 58, 83
Milton, John, 19, 69, 74, 76, 80, 81, 84,
85, 86, 90, 100, 103, 105, 111, 120,
134, 137, 146n7
Montague, Mrs. Elizabeth, 133
Morris, John N., 41
Muggletonians, 17
music, 27, 42, 63, 70, 88, 104, 105,
120–21, 137

Offor, George, 30, 81, 84, 130, 131, 133
Owen, John, 20, 27
Oxford Book of English Verse, 106

Peacham, Henry, 102
"Phyllida flouts me," 106
Ponder, Nathaniel "Bunyan," 132
Pope, Alexander, 88
Popish Plot, 108
Presbyterians, 16, 17, 21
proverbs, 42, 61, 70, 88
Prudentius, 81
puns, 13, 42, 61, 86, 104, 120, 137
Puritanism, 14, 15–19, 24, 36, 37, 38,
39, 52, 54, 57, 59, 63, 64, 65, 66, 69,
70, 71, 73, 76, 80, 81, 84, 85, 86, 87,
90, 98, 100, 101, 105, 112, 120, 123,
124, 127, 128, 135, 136, 137

Quakers, 17, 18, 19, 25, 26, 34, 40, 122,
128
Quarles, Francis, 31, 112, 118, 133

Ranters, 17, 33, 40, 42, 122
Reynolds, John, 68
Richardson, Samuel, 133
riddles, 61, 62, 88–89, 107
Roosevelt, Theodore, 135
Rowley, William, 68
Ruffhead, Josias, 25

Rupert, Prince, 30, 84
Sadler, Thomas, 148n3
Shakespeare, 62, 106, 134, 135
Sharrock, Roger, 54, 84, 100, 111
Shaw, George Bernard, 70, 81, 135, 136
S[herman], T]homas], 109
Smith, Francis "Elephant," 29
Smith, John, 17
Smith, Thomas, 20
Southey, Robert, 133
Spenser, Edmund, 16, 54, 135
Spira, Francis, 31, 34, 40
Sprat, Thomas, 133
Stevenson, Robert L., 150n3
Strudwick, John, 29
Struggler, The, 132
Sturt, John, 149n3
Suckling, Sir John, 74
Swift, Jonathan, 133

Talon, Henri, 98
Thackeray, William Makepeace, 135
Third Part of The Pilgrim's Progress,
132
"35th of Elizabeth," 22
Tillotson, John, 133
Tillyard, E. M. W., 85
Tindall, William York, 84, 134
Tolkien, J. R. R., 134
typology, 28, 29, 58, 128

Vaughan, Henry, 120
Venner, Thomas, 21

Webber, Joan, 41
White, Robert, 134
Whitney, Geoffrey, 122
Williams, Vaughan, 135
Wingate, Justice Francis, 21, 22
Wither, George, 31, 112, 128
Wycliffites, 16

DATE DUE

4/2/96			